PENANG
Nyonya Cooking

FOODS OF MY CHILDHOOD

PENANG
Nyonya Cooking

FOODS OF MY CHILDHOOD

CECILIA TAN

Times Books International
Singapore • Kuala Lumpur

Food photographs: Yim Chee Peng of Culinary Studios
Home Economist: Mrs Margaret Yim
Assistant Home Economist: Rahilah Begum
Graphics: Jennifer Chua
Design: Lim Hoon Eng

First published in 1983
Reprinted 1985, 1988, 1989, 1992, 1995

Published by Times Books International
an imprint of Times Editions Pte Ltd
Times Centre, 1 New Industrial Road
Singapore 1953

Times Subang
Lot 46, Subang Hi-Tech Industrial Park
Batu Tiga, 40000 Shah Alam
Selangor Darul Ehsan, Malaysia

Printed in Singapore

ISBN 981 204 309 8

Dedication

To See Yin, Juliana and Luisa

Acknowledgments

The publishers wish to thank
Mr Peter Wee of Katong Antique House
for the use of his beautiful antiques and also
Aw Pottery and Lim's Arts and Crafts
for their fine crockery.
Special thanks to Mr Felix Chia
for his unusual
Blanc-mange and jelly mould.

FOREWORD

In our Penang childhood, Cecilia Tan and I took good food for granted. Cecilia was the luckier — her home was a sort of crossroads where two of the world's most unique cooking styles met. With a Peranakan mother and a Hainanese father, classic meals were the norm.

As we grew up and wandered away to seek fame and fortune — Cecilia at 19 to live on her own for the first time in university — we gradually realised things weren't going to be easy. How could we swallow hamburgers when our thoughts dwelt longingly on char kway teow (fried noodles) thick with prawns, cockles and bean sprouts?

It's easy to love good food, but it takes a journalist's inquiring mind to probe its cultural mysteries. Cecilia was a journalist for eight years. One day, at a family wedding when the clan was gathered, she cornered her 48-year-old maternal aunt, doyenne of cooks in her family.

'We spent hours talking about food,' Cecilia recalls. 'She gave me her secret tips for successful cooking — like how to make your char kway teow as good as the hawker's — and the oral history of Penang nyonya cuisine.'

There is a distinct difference between Penang nyonya cuisine (called northern, because the state is north of the Malaysian peninsula) and the Singapore (southern) variety, although both sprang from the same cultural evolution — the blending of Chinese and Malay styles of cooking.

More Thai influence has crept into the sauces of the north, for example, and there are dishes not so familiar to the south, like assam laksa, Bosomboh, Penang Rojak, Heh Kian Taugeh, Acar Limau and Egg Branda, all of which you will find in this book.

Cecilia has coaxed over 150 recipes from her family, some handed down for three or four generations. This is a rare collection, organised with loving attention to detail. Each section — acars (pickles, including a special salt fish acar Cecilia's aunt has been perfecting for 30 years), gulais (curries), sambal, soups and special dishes like rojak — has an introduction in which the journalist explains the background of each type of food.

'I have a passion for food,' says Cecilia, who is no mean cook herself. 'I want to share the food of my childhood so that my children and others will know and enjoy them as well.'

Cecilia, who has a Master's degree in English Language and Literature from the Victoria University of Wellington, New Zealand, recently left a full-time job in the advertising industry to concentrate on free-lance writing. She is working on an authorised biography of a well-known local personality and — she has promised — more family recipes.

Muriel Speeden
journalist

CONTENTS

Foreword   7
Introduction   10
Ingredients in Nyonya Cooking   11
Helpful Hints   14
Weights and Measures   15

Northern Nyonya
      Specialties   17
Acars   33
Gulais   41
Sambals   53
Poultry   65
Pork   71
Seafood   79
Vegetables   91
Noodles and Rice   103
Soups   115
Kuihs & Desserts   125
Index   140

INTRODUCTION

The foods of my childhood are a treasure-house of gastronomic memories: of devoted mothers, grandmothers and household retainers who rose with the dawn to pound, stir, grind, simmer and stoke in order to prepare the labours of love that were spread on the family table daily.

Mealtimes then were grand affairs, with cuisine that delighted the palate with varying tastes, flavours and textures, while tea-time meant more melt-in-the-mouth treats. Food was cooked with an exacting skill. This was especially so in Penang nyonya households.

Northern nyonya cooking is heavily influenced by Thai cuisine because of Thailand's close proximity. The liberal use of chillies, lime juice and tamarind pulp (for that unmistakable sour, searing, hot sensation) is evidence of this.

Generally, northern nyonya cooking is hot, spicy and lemak (rich). A lot of pungent roots (lengkuas, serai, turmeric, halia), aromatic leaves (daun pandan, daun kaduk, daun pudina, daun kesum) and other ingredients like shrimp paste (belacan), dried prawns (heh bee), fresh and dried chillies, limes and tamarind paste, to name a few, are used in its cooking.

The richness of the dishes come from the generous use of coconut milk (santan) and spices. To counteract the cloy feeling, there are sour dishes which make use of tamarind paste or lime juice. This gives a good balance of tastes in meals.

Though most homes cook similar dishes, they are prepared with great variations to suit individual family tastes. This accounts for why one family's acars (pickles) are more crunchy and spicy than another's or why first aunty's gulais (curries) are not as fiery hot or tangy as third aunty's.

However, preparation was always meticulous and results delicious. Whether it was a kuih, sambal, gulai or acar, a nyonya kitchen always turned out impeccable, perfect concoctions.

Today, a lot of these foods are rarely prepared, let alone served at family meals. Our modern, hurried pace of life and lack of willing hands have led to the commercially prepared variety of nyonya food. Grandmother's wholesome, lip-smacking and hearty meals are, alas, things of the past.

A keen awareness of this (and a hankering for foods of the past) led me to put pen to paper. This is the result: a collection of the daily nyonya staples of my childhood. These recipes have been in the family for three generations or more.

Though I have selected dishes that are easily prepared (even by a novice), a lot of these recipes are family secrets; tried, tested and retested till near-perfect. Two of such special dishes are Salt-fish Acar and Limau Acar. They have undergone 30 years of experimentation and adaptation by my maternal aunt who lifted the recipes from the family's old cookery files.

Also included are quite a few less well-known recipes. These are no longer prepared regularly either because the recipes have become obscure or the ingredients are no longer readily available. Heh Kian Taugeh and Salt-fish Branda are cases in point.

I have also sneaked in a couple of recipes that are not strictly nyonya in origin but are regular foods, nonetheless, in nyonya households. Mee Rebus is one of these.

The recipes in this collection show up the differences between northern (Penang) and southern (Malacca and Singapore) nyonya cooking. Aside from the wide variety of sambals and acars that dominate northern nyonya cooking, there are also certain dishes peculiar to, and synonymous with, this cuisine. Among them are Purut Ikan (a delicacy made from fish stomach), Bosomboh (a crispy salad tossed in a thick gravy sauce), Egg Branda, Penang Rojak and Prawn Congee to name a few.

Traditional northern nyonya cooking was difficult to master in the past because standard measurements were seldom used in the kitchen. Everything was done through the agak-agak (estimation) method, where a pinch of this or a toss of that, a handful of this and a thumbful of that were the only cooking measurements at hand. Thankfully, we do not have to resort to this instinctive method of cooking today, but we do have to convert from imperial to metric. The recipes in this book incorporate standard measurements. These can be further adapted to suit personal tastes. If, for example, you prefer more fire in your sambals or a richer gravy to your gulais, make adjustments accordingly. Agak-agak till the dishes are to your satisfaction.

Bon appetit!

Cecilia Tan

INGREDIENTS IN NYONYA COOKING

Agar Agar
A local type of jelly extracted from seaweed. It sets without refrigeration. Agar agar is available in powdered form as well as clear strips. It has no natural sweetness of its own and sugar must always be added when preparing desserts with agar agar.

Candlenuts (Buah Keras)
A cream coloured, waxy and heart-shaped nut which has a thickening effect when added to dishes. They are sold shelled in South East Asian markets.

Chillies
The hottest of all peppery spices, both dried and fresh ones are used in nyonya cooking. Although the dried ones give a special flavour to a dish, it is fiery hot — so use with discretion.

From my observation, my nyonya relatives of the traditional school of cooking usually retain the seeds of the dried chillies in their cooking. If you discard the seeds, you have to add an extra two seedless dried chillies to make up for the hotness. If you do not like chilli seeds in your dish, remove them before soaking the dried chillies by cutting off either end of the chilli and shaking the seeds out.

Fresh red or green chillies are usually used for their colour. Seeds can be scraped off by making a slit on one side and scraping off with a sharp knife. Fresh chillies are usually sliced into fine rings or cut lengthwise for garnishing. Chillies can be also added to dishes a minute or two before the heat is turned off.

If you care for extra stinging hotness add some Chilli Padi (Bird's Eye Chilli). Here, the short green ones are preferable.

Coconut Milk (Santan)
The richness of nyonya dishes, whether in curries or desserts, come from the prevalent use of santan or coconut milk. It is this creamy, thick, white milk that gives the rich, full-bodied (and very satisfying) taste to curries, sauces, rice dishes, desserts and kuihs.

To obtain the best results, wrap the grated coconut in a piece of clean muslin cloth, twisting it to extract the milk. This milk is called pati or first santan. One rice bowl of water to 1½ rice bowls of grated coconut should yield a rich consistency. For extra coconut milk, called second santan, add a little more water to the grated coconut and squeeze again.

Since santan is sensitive to high heat, any cooking with coconut milk as an ingredient should be done under regulated, moderate heat. The dish should also be constantly stirred when it comes to the boil or the coconut milk will curdle. Santan should never be overcooked. Signs of overcooking are that it will become thick and oil will begin to appear. If overcooked, the santan will change into oil and leave a deposit at the bottom of the pan.

Coriander Leaves
Mainly used as a garnish as one would use parsley, coriander leaves are delicate and lacy. Known as Wan Swee to Chinese cooks, it has a distinctive flavour which is less pronounced in younger leaves.

Curry Leaves
South Indian in origin, curry leaves are used mainly in curries. Each leaflet is about 2.5 cm long and are opposite one another. They are dark green in colour and are slightly glossy when cleaned.

Daun Limau Purut
This is the leaf of a variety of citrus. Discriptive names include wrinkled lime and leperous lime. Having its origin in Thailand, the leaves have a subtle fragrance which gives a distinctive taste to many Nyonya foods. The small variety of daun limau purut have leaves about 4 cm long while the large variety may have leaves as big as a child's palm.

Dried Prawns (Udang Kering)
Used frequently in sambals, vegetable dishes and soups, they need to be soaked and well drained before cooking. Do not use too much water or soak them for too long or the prawns will become tasteless. The water should just cover the dried prawns when soaking. Nyonyas often use the water in which Dried Prawns have been soaked in their cooking (strain first). When used in any dish, Dried Prawns give a pleasantly strong flavour that whets the appetite.

Five Spice Powder (Ng Heong Fun)
A ground combination of star anise, fennel seeds, cloves, cinnamon and peppercorns. Five Spice Powder is available from most grocery shops and Chinese medical halls. This fragrant seasoning ingredient is popular as a marinade.

Fresh Shrimp Fry (Gerago)

These are tiny shrimps which are used in omelettes and as the main ingredient for Chinchalok. It is a seasonal seafood and can be difficult to obtain in inland areas.

Fried and Pounded Grated Coconut (Krisek)

Freshly grated coconut is fried over a very low fire till brown. It is then pounded finely. In the pounding process, the coconut will increase in volume. Krisek is usually used in kerabu dishes — recipes that call for a combination of various ingredients which are mixed well before serving. Examples are Nasi Ulam and Jantung Pisang Kerabu.

Galangal (Lengkuas)

A ginger-like root which is creamy white in colour. It has a delicate flavour.

Golden Needles (Kim Chiam)

These are dried yellow fungus which are about eight centimetres long. It is prepared by soaking in warm water to soften it before the hard tips are cut off. They are often knotted up before cooking. Mainly used in soups, it has a strong, fragrant flavour.

Lemon Grass (Serai)

Giving a very strong pungent flavour, Lemon Grass is used liberally in most curry-based dishes. The end of the stalk (about seven centimetres from the root end) is usually cut off. It is used sliced, pounded or bruised.

Limes

Limau, which is the lemon-shaped variety of lime used in nyonya cooking is larger than its cousin, limau kasturi. This smaller lime is round and more fragrant. It is the juice of this little lime that gives Sambal Belacan its kick.

Nutmeg (Buah Pala)

Nutmeg is a hard, dark and aromatic kernal fruit of the nutmeg tree. It is a pungent spice so use with discretion. Nutmeg should be grated into a dish when required although powdered nutmeg can also be used.

Palm Sugar (Gula Melaka)

The best palm sugar is reputed to come from Malacca, the stronghold of Baba culture which lends its name to this ingredient. It is made from the sap of the coconut flower and sold in cylinderical blocks traditionally wrapped in dried coconut fronds. It is dark brown in colour.

Polygonum (Daun Kesom)

This is a dark green herb with a pungent flavour often used in northern nyonya cooking.

Prawn Paste (Heh Koh)

This is a thick black paste which has to be diluted before use. It's odour and taste are thought to be pungent and powerful to the uninitiated. A delicacy of sorts, its use is actually limited to a few specialties like Penang Assam Laksa and Rojak. However, it can be used as a dip for chillies, cucumbers and mangoes. Without Heh Koh, the dishes mentioned above lose their hallmark.

Salted Cabbage

Chinese white cabbage is pickled in salt partially dried to make Salted Cabbage. It can be obtained in local markets or as a canned food in supermarkets.

Screwpine Leaves (Daun Pandan)

Screwpine Leaves give a distinctive fragrance to desserts and kuihs. They are usually torn lengthwise down the middle (to release the fragrance) and knotted loosely before being used in cooking. The plant can be easily grown in backyards.

Sesame Seeds (Mua Chi)

These tiny seeds give a nutty flavour and crunchy texture to dishes. They are usually toasted or fried before use and mainly sprinkled over dishes or used in snacks.

Shrimp Paste (Belacan)

A regular ingredient in local cooking, shrimp paste most often appears on nyonya dining tables as Sambal Belacan which is served with lime juice and used as a dip.

Slaked Lime (Kapor)

This ingredient is not derived from either lime plant or kapok tree but is a paste obtained by grinding sea shells in a little liquid. This is the lime which is chewed with betel nuts, betel leaves, gambier and Javanese tobacco by the Babas and Malays.

Soya Beans

This bean is of high nutritional value and a rich, cheap source of vegetable protein. Indigenous to the Orient, it appears in a wide variety of cake-forms. Among them are soya bean cake, soft soya bean cake which is used braised or in soups, fried spongy soya bean cubes, soya bean strips and dried sweet soya bean curd.

Soya Bean Paste (Taucheong)

This is a thick paste made from black or yellow beans and mixed with flour and salt. It is sold in jars in its preserved form. Soya Bean Paste is salty and should not be used too liberally. Do not add salt to a dish when this ingredient is used.

Tamarind Pulp (Assam Jawa)
Tamarind Pieces (Assam Keping)

These come from the pods of the tamarind tree. The pulp is a sticky, fibrous mass with broken seed pods. To obtain the tamarind liquid, this is usually squeezed in a little hot water and then strained. The liquid is then added to the dish. Tamarind pieces are often used in place of pulp. One or two of them are added to the dish and discarded when the food has attained the required sourness. Both these ingredients are invaluable in the preparation of some curries.

Transparent Vermicelli (Tung Hoon)

Sold in its dehydrated form, Transparent Vermicelli is very popularly used in soups and stir-fried with vegetables. It is soaked in warm water and cut into shorter lengths before cooking.

Turmeric (Kunyit)

An essential root in nyonya cooking, its flavour and yellow colour makes meat, fish and pickle dishes distinctive.

Yambean (Sengkuang)

Also known locally as Bangkuang, this is a top-shaped tuber. Its sandy brown skin is discarded and the white crunchy interior is served as a vegetable.

HELPFUL HINTS IN THE KITCHEN

The round bottomed kuali or iron wok is the most useful utensil when cooking in a nyonya kitchen. This large, wide-mouthed, deep pan is ideal because it can accommodate all kinds of cooking, whether it be deep-frying, stir-frying, steaming or stewing. You can, of course, use any other suitable type of frying pan.

A thinner version of the kuali is recommended for frying rice, kuih teow, mee and vegetables. This is what gives that special taste found in foods prepared by hawkers. The secret lies in heat coming faster through the thinner kuali and thus the ingredients do not have the tendency to stick to the sides (as it does in the thicker, regular kuali). The taste and the finish of the dish therefore, comes out better.

While gulais (curries) are usually cooked in an Indian clay pot, those with a steady hand can use the regular kuali for the same purpose without sacrificing taste. For soups, the traditional nyonya cook used a gnah phoh (enamel pot) for both boiling and simmering.

Pounding and Grinding

For pounding and grinding of spices and roots, the traditional way was to use the batu lesong (mortar and pestle) and the batu giling (grinding stone and roller).

The batu lesong is used for pounding sambal belacan, dried prawns, groundnuts, onions, chillies, dried chillies and serai. The batu giling is used when the rempah includes spices like ketumbar (coriander), jintan putih (fennel seeds) and jintan manis (cummin seeds). Grinding this way is easier and quicker than pounding with pestle and mortar and you also get a finer paste. In the modern kitchen, the blender or grinder is, of course, the handiest way to prepare sambals or spices. The cooks of the old school, however, swear that taste is sacrificed for convenience.

Another indispensible utensil in a nyonya kitchen is the parut. Used for grating coconut, tapioca, fresh ginger, carrot, potato and the like, it is usually a metal sheet perforated with holes of various sizes. To parut, therefore, means to grate or shred.

Roots and spices to be fried in a rempah or paste are usually prepared and pounded in the following order:
1. Kunyit (turmeric) thinly sliced or shredded.
2. Serai (lemon grass) cut into small pieces or sliced finely.
3. Dried chillies, soaked in warm water for 15 minutes*.
4. Toasted belacan (shrimp paste).
5. Fresh chillies, sliced†.
6. Shallots.
7. Garlic.

Each ingredient should be pounded finely before the next ingredient to be pounded is added. Fresh and dried chillies are usually pounded together; so too, garlic and onions. Onions and garlic are usually added last because they give out more liquid.

* Remove seeds before soaking in warm water. Tear open the ends and shake the dried seeds out if a very hot dish is not preferred.
† Remove seeds before pounding by slicing sides and removing with a sharp knife. If you prefer a hotter dish, do not remove the seeds and add chilli padi (bird's eye chilli).

Frying a Rempah

An Indian claypot or belanga is ideal for frying a rempah. A kuali can be used to good effect as well, provided heat is well controlled and low. If care is not taken, the rempah will either dry out, get stuck to the bottom of the pan or get burnt.

Oil for frying should always be hot before any ingredients are added. It is always important that rempah is well stirred, fragrant and bubbling in enough oil before other ingredients are added. If it shows a tendency to dry up, add a little extra oil or coconut milk and stir well. In nyonya cooking, the way a rempah is fried is what counts most as it contributes directly to a well cooked dish.

Note of interest

The nyonyas had their own cooking terms such as tumis, kembang and wajek-wajek. To avoid confusion, I have omitted the use of these terms in the recipes and have substituted them with the following:

Tumis: To fry till fragrant.

Kembang: To expand in volume or size.

Wajek-wajek: To cut or slice at a slant. Popularly employed in cutting vegetables.

Rempah: Mixture of ground or pounded ingredients.

WEIGHTS AND MEASURES

Metric measurements are used throughout this book. For liquids, the rice bowl is used. This is the standard Chinese porcelain bowl used for serving rice. The equivalent is seven fluid ounces or 200 millilitres of liquid.

Where a recipe calls for seasoning or Monosodium Glutamate (which is optional), a pinch is more than enough. Where a recipe recommends that chilli seeds be discarded, you could do otherwise if you so prefer.

The measurements in this book are very close guides. Salt and sugar measures for dishes should be adjusted accordingly to personal tastes. The same goes for tamarind paste or pieces. Remember that the longer these souring agents stay in a dish, the more sour the dish will be.

Abbreviations used in this book are as follows:

tbsp — tablespoon
tsp — teaspoonful
cm — centimetres
g — grammes
kg — kilogrammes

Metric equivalents are as follows:

1 oz — 30 g
2 oz — 60 g
3 oz — 90 g
4 oz — 120 g
5 oz — 150 g
6 oz — 180 g
7 oz — 210 g
½ lb — 250 g
1 lb — 500 g
2 lb — 1 kg

2 tahs — 75 g
4 tahs — 150 g
½ kati — 300 g
1 kati — 600 g

Northern Nyonya Specialities

To the nyonya of old, cooking was an accomplishment, an art to be proud of. It was with pride that she applied her skills in the never-ending daily task of preparing food. Her efforts were not in vain, for northern nyonya cuisine can boast of dishes exclusive to it.

As always, it was the nyonya cook's innovative experimentation that cooked up winners like Bosomboh, Penang Rojak, Nyonya Chang, Lobak, Stuffed Taukua, Purut Ikan and Egg Branda.

In their own right, these dishes have become very special, for they are so versatile that they can be eaten as an appetizer, a snack, a side dish or even as a meal by themselves. The nyonyas have their own terms for such dishes; chia thit tho, literally meaning 'eating for the sheer enjoyment or pleasure derived from it', whatever the time of day, whatever the occasion or time of year.

BOSOMBOH
(Nyonya Salad)

This delicious way of serving a salad must have been borrowed from the Indians generations ago. Whereas Bosomboh is the Indian-Malay name for the dish, the Nyonya call their version 'Cheh Hu' which translates into 'Green Fish'. This is possibly because of the green seaweed that is sometimes added to the dish. Bosomboh and the seaweed have now disappeared from street stalls and family tables. It is hoped that this recipe, which was coaxed from an old and expert hand at preparing the dish, will return Bosomboh to its place of popularity.

225 g prawns, shelled, cleaned and drained
250 g flour
1 cucumber, cleaned, shredded
1 yambean (sengkuang), skinned, washed, shredded
300 g beansprouts, scalded in boiling water
3 pieces soya bean cake (taukua), fried till brown, cut into pieces
150 g fresh cuttlefish, boiled in water till cooked
150 g groundnuts, fried in low heat, stirring continuously for about ½ hour till brown
75 g sesame seeds, fried in low heat till brown
Baking powder
Rice flour

SAUCE INGREDIENTS
8 dried chillies, soaked in warm water for 15 minutes, drained and pounded finely
8 shallots, pounded finely
4 pips garlic, pounded finely
4 tbsp sugar
1 tbsp light soya sauce
1 tbsp tamarind paste (assam jawa), dissolved in 2½ rice bowls of water, strained
1 tbsp corn flour, mixed well in 3 tbsp water
½ tsp salt
9 tbsp cooking oil

PREPARATION

1. Place in a big round serving plate shredded cucumber, yambean, beansprouts, cut fried soya bean cake and cut cooked cuttlefish.
2. Pound groundnuts coarsely after letting it cool and removing skin. Set aside.

Prawn Fritters
1. Mince 225 g prawns.
2. Add flour, 1 teaspoonful rice flour, ¾ level teaspoon baking powder.
3. Add water slowly, stirring until it becomes a batter. Beat till smooth. The batter should be of a thick consistency. Set aside.

METHOD

1. Heat kuali, add oil for deep frying. When oil is hot, deep fry tablespoons of batter till brown. Reduce heat to low so that it will not overheat quickly.
2. Dish out. Drain, cool and cut into slices.

Sauce
1. Dish out all but 9 tablespoonfuls of oil from the pan.
2. Add pounded shallots and garlic. Stir a few seconds and add pounded chillies and 3 tablespoons water. Stir until fragrant.
3. Add tamarind juice, sugar and salt. Slow boil until sugar dissolves.
4. Add 1 tablespoon light soya sauce to corn flour. Mix well.
5. Stir in briskly till the gravy starts to thicken. If insufficiently thick, add more dissolved corn flour or pounded groundnuts.

To Serve
Place cucumber, yambean, beansprouts, soya bean cake, cuttlefish and prawn fritters into a serving dish. Sprinkle some groundnuts and sesame seeds on top. Add gravy and serve.

BOSOMBOH: A light spicy salad ideal for a sultry Penang afternoon.

PENANG ROJAK
(Penang Salad)

1 medium-sized cucumber
1 medium-sized yambean (sengkuang)
2 young mangoes
A few guavas (jambu air)
1 small pineapple
2 pieces soya bean cake (taukua)
150 g fresh cuttlefish
10 dried chillies
1 rice bowl of sweet black sauce (t'nee choew)
3 tbsp shrimp paste (belacan)
3 tbsp black prawn paste (heh koh)
30 – 40 g sesame seeds
150 g groundnuts
black soya sauce
light soya sauce
sugar to taste

PREPARATION

1. Fry soya bean cake.
2. Boil cuttlefish for a few minutes until cooked.
3. Heat shrimp paste in a pan, crumble. Fry until dry and fragrant.
4. Pound chillies finely. Add a little hot water and stir into a fairly thick solution.
5. Fry groundnuts in pan at low heat, stir continuously until fairly brown.
6. Mix black prawn paste with a little hot water and stir to mix well.
7. Fry sesame seeds in a pan at very low heat until fairly brown. Care should be taken as they burn easily.
8. Heat sweet red sauce in a pan at low heat. Add a little water; boil into a fairly thick solution.
9. Pound the fried groundnuts coarsely.

METHOD

1. Cut the following into bite-sized pieces: cucumber, yambean, mangoes, guavas, pineapple, fried soya bean cake and boiled cuttlefish.
2. Put a little of each of the above into a bowl. Add 4 table-spoons sweet red sauce, 1 teaspoon black prawn paste, 1 teaspoon chillie paste, 2 tablespoons sugar, a few drops black soya sauce and 1 teaspoon white soya sauce and 1 teaspoon shrimp paste. Stir and mix well.
3. Pour into a plate, garnish with sesame seeds and groundnuts. Serve.

Note:
No water is to be added.

GADO GADO

150 g water convolvulus
100 g long beans
100 g beansprouts
1 small cucumber
1 small yambean (sengkuang)
2 pieces soya bean cake (taukua)
2 hard boiled eggs
1 potato
150 g groundnuts
½ coconut, grated
5 tbsp sugar
6 tbsp cooking oil
½ tsp salt

SAUCE INGREDIENTS
2 tbsp coriander (ketumbar), ground finely
Thumb-sized piece fresh young turmeric (kunyit), skinned
5 shallots
3 pips garlic

PREPARATION

1. Snip off leaves and young stems from water convolvulus. Cut vegetable into 5 centimetre lengths. Clean, drain in water and scald in boiling water until soft. Set aside.
2. Cut off long bean tips, and cut the bean into 5 centimetre lengths. Boil till cooked. Set aside.
3. Remove beansprout roots, clean, wash and drain. Scald in boiling water till soft but still crispy.
4. Clean, skin and shred cucumber and yambean.
5. Fry soya bean cakes and cut into cubes.
6. Shell eggs and slice into pieces.
7. Boil potato till cooked. Remove skin and cut into bite-size pieces.
8. Fry groundnuts at low heat till fairly brown. Cool, remove skin and pound coursely. Set aside.
9. Add 1¼ rice bowl of water to coconut and squeeze for milk.

METHOD

1. Heat pan then add oil. Add all sauce ingredients except coriander. Stir for a moment then add coriander. Stir well till fragrant.
2. Add coconut milk, salt and sugar. Stir till sugar is dissolved. Add pounded groundnuts. Stir for a minute. Remove from heat and dish out.
3. Serve vegetables, soya bean cake and egg in individual bowls. Pour gravy on top.

NYONYA KIAM T'NEE CHANG
(Nyonya rice dumplings)

'Chang' or rice-dumplings are made from glutinous rice with sweet or savoury fillings, wrapped in bamboo leaves and shaped into small pyramids. The 'kiam t'nee' (savoury/sweet) 'chang' is a traditional nyonya speciality.

500 g glutinous rice
150 g preserved sugared melon pieces
150 g groundnuts
225 g streaky pork
2½ tbsp coriander (ketumbar)
1½ cm cekur/sar keong
30 white peppercorns
5 shallots
4 pips garlic
1 tsp light soya sauce
1 tsp dark soya sauce
3 tbsp sugar
3 tbsp lard
3 – 4 rice bowls of cooking oil
Sugar and salt to taste
225 g bamboo leaves
75 g hemp

PREPARATION

1. Soak the glutinous rice in water for 4 hours, clean and drain.
2. Mince preserved sugared melon pieces.
3. Fry groundnuts at low heat until brown, stirring continuously. After frying, cool and remove skin, then pound coarsely.
4. Boil streaky pork till cooked, mince.
5. Grind coriander, peppercorns and cekur finely. Pound shallots and garlic finely.
6. Wash leaves and hemp thoroughly. Dip in boiling water to soften.

METHOD

1. Heat pan, add cooking oil till hot. Add pounded onions and garlic and ground coriander mixture. Stir until fragrant.
2. Reduce heat to medium and add minced pork, minced preserved sugared melon, dark and light soya sauce, sugar and salt to taste. The ingredients should taste slightly sweet and a little saltish. Stir until the pork is cooked and sugar is dissolved. No water is to be added.
3. Steam the glutinous rice for 25 minutes, remove and mix well with the lard and a little salt.
4. Fold the middle of a leaf to form a cone.

Fill cone with glutinous rice, make a well in the centre to stuff with the fried ingredients. Cover with rice, then fold the leaf to make a pyramid-shaped dumpling. Secure firmly with hemp.

5. Tie rice dumplings into bundles of 6 – 8 tightly with hemp. Steam for 35 minutes. Remove and serve.

Note:
Do not boil the dumplings.

PORK AND CHESTNUT DUMPLINGS

1 kg glutinous rice
600 g belly pork
225 g green peas
125 g mushrooms
2 – 3 tbsp dark soya sauce
225 g shelled Chinese chestnuts
1½ tsp salt
½ tsp sugar
1 tsp five spice powder
1 tbsp Chinese wine
½ tsp borax (pung sar)
300 g bamboo leaves
75 g hemp

PREPARATION

1. Wash glutinous rice and soak overnight. Drain and rub in some dark soya sauce and borax.
2. Cut pork into 4 centimeter cubes.
3. Wash and half chestnuts.
4. Cut mushrooms into pieces after soaking for a while in a little water.
5. Mix all the above ingredients with 2 tablespoonfuls dark soya sauce, salt, five spice powder and sugar. Leave aside for ½ hour to 45 minutes.

METHOD

1. Overlap two bamboo leaves. Shape into a cone and spoon glutinous rice into it. Make a well in the rice and fill with marinated ingredients and some green peas.
2. Cover ingredients with rice and fold leaf to form a pyramid-shaped dumpling. Secure firmly with hemp.
3. Tie individual dumplings into bunches of 6 to 8. Boil for 4 – 4½ hours.

OTAK OTAK

300 g fish fillets
1 coconut, grated
3 A-sized eggs
2–3 bundles daun kaduk
6 daun limau purut
1 stalk lemon grass
8 shallots
1 tsp shrimp paste (belacan)
Thumb-sized piece fresh turmeric (kunyit)
4 fresh red chillies
1 tsp pepper
3 tbsp coriander (ketumbar), ground finely
Banana leaves

PREPARATION

1. Grind coriander finely.
2. Grind together shallots, lemon grass, daun limau purut, shrimp paste, chillies and tumeric till fine.
3. Cut fish fillets into slices. Clean, wash and drain.
4. Remove stalks of daun kaduk, wash and drain.
5. Add 2½ rice bowls of water to grated coconut and squeeze to extract milk.
6. Soak banana leaves in hot water till soft. Remove, cool and clean with a cloth. Cut into pieces of 20 cm square for wrapping fish mixture.
7. Put the ground ingredients into a container. Break in 3 eggs, and ½ teaspoonful salt and slowly pour in the coconut milk. Stir well until it becomes a thick paste. Add fish and mix well.

METHOD

1. Put 3 or 4 daun kaduk leaves in the centre of a banana leaf. Scoop about 4 tablespoonfuls of the mixed ingredients on top of the daun kaduk. Lift two sides of the banana leaf and fold towards the centre. Do the same with the other ends to make a package. Hold package in place with staples or the mid-rib of a coconut leaf.
2. Repeat till all the ingredients are used up.
3. Place packages on the steaming tray and steam for about 8 to 10 minutes. Remove and serve.

Note:
An alternative to wrapping the Otak Otak in banana leaves is to put mixed ingredients directly into a steaming tray and steam.

In this recipe, the daun limau purut is pounded and not sliced. Though colour is sacrificed (it turns a slightly dirty green), the taste of the Otak Otak is without a leafy tartness and therefore, better.

ROTI BABI

6 slices overnight bread
2 eggs

STUFFING INGREDIENTS
100 g pork
1 tbsp coriander (ketumbar)
10 peppercorns
¾ inch cekur/sar keong
1 tsp dark soya sauce
1 tsp light soya sauce
4 shallots
2 pips garlic
¼ tsp salt
Monosodium glutamate/seasoning (optional)
5 tbsp cooking oil
2 tsp flour

PREPARATION

1. Grind coriander, peppercorns and cekur finely.
2. Pound shallots and garlic finely.
3. Mince pork finely.
4. Beat eggs in a little flour.
5. Make deep slits along the sides of the bread using a sharp knife.

METHOD

1. Heat 5 tablespoonfuls of cooking oil. When hot, add pounded onions and garlic and fry till soft. Add pounded coriander, peppercorns and cekur as well as dark and light soya sauces.
2. Stir over low heat until fragrant. Add minced pork and stir until cooked.
3. Dish out and stuff bread with mixture.
4. Heat 1½ rice bowls of oil till hot. Dip both sides of the bread in the beaten egg and fry at low heat until both sides are slightly brown.
5. Dish out, drain oil and serve.

Note:
Overnight bread is used because fresh bread is too soft to make the slits for stuffing.

HEH KIAN TAUGEH
(Beansprouts and Prawn Fritters)

This dish is little known, having almost been lost with time. A very old relative still cooks this and the recipe is said to be four to five generations old.

225 g beansprouts
150 g fresh prawns
8 tbsp flour
½ tsp baking powder
10 tbsp water
2 rice bowls oil
Salt to taste

PREPARATION

1. Bruise beansprouts with fingers. Set aside.
2. Shell, wash and drain prawns. Mince.
3. Add minced prawns, salt, flour, baking powder and water to mashed beansprouts.
4. Mix well till batter is smooth.

METHOD

1. Heat oil in frying pan.
2. Deep fry mixture in spoonfuls. The fritters must be thin and about 4–5 centimeters in diameter.
3. Serve with chilli sauce and rice. (See FRIED TAUKUA at page 26 for chilli sauce recipe).

Note:
Yambean may be used instead of beansprouts for this dish. A variation omits prawns in the recipe.

HEH KIAH
(Prawn Fritters)

100 g shelled prawns, minced
15 tbsp flour, sieved
14 tbsp water
1 level tsp baking powder
1 level tsp pepper
1 B-sized egg
1 tsp light soya sauce
½ tsp salt
¼ big onion, minced
Monosodium glutamate/seasoning (optional)
Cooking oil
1 chilli, finely sliced (optional)

METHOD

1. Put minced prawns into a big bowl. Add pepper, monosodium glutamate, salt and light soya sauce. Stir well to mix.
2. Add flour, baking powder, onion, chilli, egg and a few tablespoonfuls of water at a time. Stir until it becomes a soft batter.
3. Set aside for 10 – 15 minutes.
4. Heat enough oil in frying pan. Put about ¾ tablespoon of the batter into hot oil. Deep fry.
5. Adjust heat from medium to low so that there will be no overheating or burning. Fry fritters till light brown and remove to a metal sieve to drain the oil.
6. Remove excess oil with kitchen paper towels. Serve, with a sambal and sliced soya bean cake (taukua).

BETIK MASAK TITEK
(Papaya in Hot Gravy)

300 g half-ripe papaya
50 g dried prawns
3 shallots
1 tsp shrimp paste
2 fresh red chillies
½ tsp pepper
Salt to taste
Chicken flavouring (optional)

PREPARATION

1. Skin papaya and cut into thin slices.
2. Clean, wash and drain dried prawns.
3. Slit chillies and remove seeds.
4. Pound shallots finely.

METHOD

1. Into 3½ rice bowls of water, add pounded shallots, 1 teaspoonful shrimp paste, ½ teaspoon pepper, dried prawns, salt to taste and chicken flavouring (optional).
2. Bring to boil. Then add cut papaya, chillies. Reduce heat to medium.
3. Boil till papaya becomes soft. Remove from heat and serve.

Note:
Winter Melon (tang kua) is a substitute for papaya in this dish.

CHILLI SAUCE FOR FRIED STUFFED TAUKUA

4 red chillies
4 pips garlic
Tomato sauce
1 tsp vinegar
2 tbsp sugar
1 tsp salt

METHOD

1. Pound chillies and garlic finely.
2. Heat frying pan. Add 2 tablespoonfuls water and pounded ingredients.
3. When ingredients come to a boil, add tomato sauce, vinegar, sugar and salt.
4. Bring to boil again and remove from heat.

JANTUNG PISANG KERABU

300 g banana bud centres
Dried prawn sambal (See page 57)
1½ tbsp grated coconut

PREPARATION

1. Peel banana bud removing all layers of purple skin and yellow flowers till you see the pinkish-white heart of the bud. Cut this into four and boil in 2 rice bowls of water until banana bud is cooked. Slice into small pieces at a slant. Set aside.
2. Pound a dried prawn sambal using 30 – 40 g toasted shrimp paste.
3. Fry grated coconut on very low heat till it turns brown. Remove and pound finely. Set aside.

METHOD

1. Mix banana bud centre, fried grated coconut and dried prawn sambal. Add salt, pepper and a generous squeeze of lime to taste. Serve.

Note:

1½ tablespoon of grated coconut may seem very little but pounding it expands its volume so do not add more.

A variation of this recipe is to use the whole banana bud. Boil the whole bud till soft. Cut it lengthwise and remove flowers and banana bud centre by peeling off the purple skin. Pinch off tips and remove bony stamens of flowers. Combine with centres, grated coconut and sambal.

JANTUNG PISANG KERABU: The lowly banana bud is used ingeniously here to produce an unusual salad. It is served with banana flowers in this version. Kim Chiam or dried yellow fungus is a substitute for jantung pisang.

LOBAK: A delightful combination of texture and taste.

LOBAK
(Nyonya Meat Rolls)

Lobak or Chun Piah is a meat based version of Po Piah (which is yambean based), using bean curd sheets instead of a flour and egg crepe for wrapping the filling. Restaurants today, serve a dish which is a cross between the Po Piah and Lobak using the Po Piah skin and a mixed yambean and meat filling. This is listed on the menu as Chun Piah but experts will tell you that this is merely a watered down version of the authentic dish.

600 g shoulder pork
1 piece bean curd sheet (tau pei/ fu pei)
1 small leek
1 egg
1 tsp five spice powder
1 tsp light soya sauce
1 tsp sesame oil
1 tsp dark soya sauce
Salt to taste

PREPARATION

1. Mince the pork but not too finely.
2. Slice the leek finely.

METHOD

1. Add sliced leek, egg, five spice powder, light and dark soya sauces and salt to pork and mix well. No water is to be used.
2. Assess the number of squares of bean curd sheets you need for the amount of seasoned pork and cut the sheet accordingly.
3. Place pork on a square of bean curd sheet and slowly wrap it up. Seal the two ends by pressing together, alternatively, fold in the ends before roll-wrapping.
4. Heat pot or frying pan. Add enough oil to fry Lobak. When oil is hot, fry Lobak until brown. Drain in a metal seive.
5. Serve sliced.

SALTED DUCK EGGS

10 fresh large duck eggs
900 g coarse or rock salt
1 piece durian husk
Pickling bottle or jar large enough to contain all the
    eggs

PREPARATION

1. Boil salt in 6 – 7 rice bowls of water till dissolved. Cool.
2. Dry durian husk in the sun. Burn and collect 2 table-
    spoonfuls of ash.

METHOD

1. Put eggs and durian husk ash into pickling jar.
2. Strain salt solution into jar until eggs are covered
    completely. Cover the jar, leaving a small gap for air
    to circulate.
3. Store in a cool place for three weeks.
4. To test if they are ready and to your taste, remove one
    egg and boil in water for 10 – 15 minutes. Taste. If not
    salty enough, continue pickling.

Note:
The durian husk ash causes the yolk to turn a beautiful
yellowish-red. If durian husks are unavailable, omit the ash.
   Make sure that the salt solution is cooled for 24 hours. It is
best if left for two days before eggs are pickled in it. This will
turn out beautiful yolks.

SALTED CHICKEN EGGS

10 fresh A-sized eggs
1 kg coarse or rock salt

PREPARATION

1. Dissolve salt in 6 – 7 rice bowl of water by boiling.
    Stand for at least 24 hours.

METHOD

1. Put eggs into a large pickling jar.
2. Strain the salt solution into the jar until all the eggs are
    completely covered. Cover the jar, leaving a small
    gap for circulation.
3. Store in a cool place for 18 days.
4. Test by removing and boiling an egg in hot water till
    cooked. Taste. If insufficiently salty, continue pickling.

FRIED STUFFED TAUKUA
(Fried Stuffed Soya Bean Cake)

INGREDIENTS
225 g prawns
1 handful beansprouts
6 pieces soya bean cakes (taukua)
120 g flour
1 egg
Salt
Pepper
Oil for deep frying

PREPARATION

1. Shell prawns, wash and drain.
2. Cut soya bean cakes diagonally into two, then make
    a deep slit for stuffing.
3. Wash beansprouts and cut into 2.5 cm. lengths.
4. Beat egg.
5. Put prawn and cut beansprouts into a fairly big bowl,
    add 120 g flour, ½ teaspoon salt, ½ teaspoon pepper
    and the beaten egg, stir well.

METHOD

1. Stuff the mixed ingredients into the soya bean cakes
    and put into hot oil for deep frying.
2. Reduce heat to medium or low, turn over the soya
    bean cakes often until brown and cooked. Dish out
    and drain the oil.
3. Serve with chilli sauce or tomato sauce.

Note:
If there is left over stuffing add ½ teaspoon baking powder
and stir well. Then scoop tablespoonfuls of the mixture and
deep fry in hot oil. Fry till brown, remove, drain oil and serve.

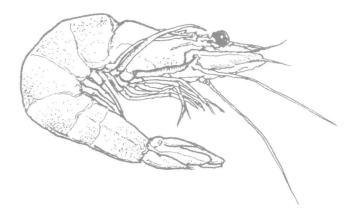

KIAM HU BRANDA
(Salt Fish Branda)

Like Egg Branda this is a very old authentic nyonya recipe that was uncovered after much research. An 84 year old distant relative still cooks this delicious and much 'endangered' dish which dates back four generations. Kiam Hu Branda is served with rice.

75 g salt fish flesh
1 big red onion
2 fresh red chillies
1 level tsp shrimp paste (belacan)
½ tbsp tamarind paste (assam jawa)
Pepper
1 tbsp sugar
Monosodium glutamate/seasoning (optional)
Dash of light soya sauce

PREPARATION

1. Soak salt fish in water for a few minutes. Drain and slice finely.
2. Cut big onion into 4 or 5 pieces after slicing the head off.
3. Slice chillies into 2 or 3 pieces lengthwise.
4. Add 1 rice bowl of water to tamarind paste and strain. Set juice aside.

METHOD

1. Fry salt fish in sufficient hot oil. When cooked, dish out fish. Remove oil.
2. Add 3 tablespoonfuls of fresh oil to frying pan. When oil is hot fry onions till transparent.
3. Add shrimp paste and crumble it when frying.
4. When shrimp paste is fragrant, add chillies, sugar and tamarind juice. Stir and taste for sweetness.
5. Add monosodium glutamate, fried salt fish, pepper and dash of light soya sauce. Serve with rice.

Note:
The sweetness in the dish should be a subtle one, so do not add too much sugar.

LA-LA FRIED IN TAUCHEONG
(Mussels in Soya bean Paste)

600 g mussels (la-la)
1½ tsp preserved soya bean paste (taucheong)
Thumb-sized piece garlic
1 fresh red chilli
5 shallots
3 pips garlic
5 tbsp cooking oil

PREPARATION

1. Soak mussels in water for 15 minutes. Remove bad ones. Wash and drain well in a colander.
2. Pound chilli finely.
3. Shred ginger.
4. Cut shallots into slices and mince garlic.

METHOD

1. Heat pan. Add oil and when hot, add garlic, ginger and onions. Fry till soft.
2. Add preserved soya bean paste and chilli. Fry till fragrant.
3. Add mussels, stir well then add ½ rice bowl of water, ½ teaspoonful light soya sauce and ½ teaspoon sugar.
4. Fry mussels till the shells open and turn red.
5. Dish out and serve.

PO PIAH
(Spring Rolls)

150 g Po Piah Skin
300 g yambean (sengkuang)
150 g pork
150 g prawns
225 g crab meat
2 pieces soya bean cake (taukua)
2 eggs
15 shallots
5 fresh red chillies
2 pips garlic, minced
1 or 2 bunches local lettuce (sang choi)
Sweet black sauce
Salt to taste

PREPARATION

1. Skin, wash and shred yambean.
2. Boil pork in some water till cooked. Remove, cool and shred.
3. Shell and clean prawns. Mince
4. Cut soya bean cakes into pieces and shred. Deep fry
5. Beat eggs, add a little flour and mix well. Heat kuali, add 3 tablespoonfuls of oil. When oil is hot, pour in half of the beaten eggs, reduce heat and swivel the kuali briskly to make a thin omelette. Turn omelette when lightly browned. Remove, cool and shred.
6. Slice shallots and deep fry until brown.
7. Pound chillies finely, add water and stir until mixture thickens.
8. Clean lettuce. Drain.

METHOD

For Filling

1. Heat a pot, then add 2 tablespoonfuls of cooking oil. Add minced garlic, stir for a few seconds then add pork and prawns. Stir for ½ minute, then add yambean. Stir till yambean is soft.
2. Add some water for a little gravy and salt to taste. Simmer for 10 minutes and remove from heat.

To Serve

Place 2 pieces of Po Pia Skin on a flat surface. Using a teaspoon, spread a little sweet black sauce and chilli sauce on the skin. Top that with 1 or 2 lettuce leaves. Using a tablespoon, scoop some filling, taking care to drain the gravy. Place filling on top of the lettuce. Add crab meat and soya bean cake, egg and fried onions. Fold sides inwards and roll-wrap into elongated shape. Cut into 4 pieces and place on a plate. Add 1 or 2 tablespoons gravy on top of the Spring Roll and serve.

Note:
If you like a lightly crispy topping, garnish Spring Roll with half a teaspoonful of fried sliced onions.

Topping the Spring Roll with a dash or two of chilli sauce and black prawn paste will give it an unusual hot-saltish taste.

PO PIAH CHIEN
(Deep-fried Spring Rolls)

Ingredients as in PO PIAH

METHOD

1. Follow instruction for PO PIAH but do not cut or garnish the roll.
2. Fill a heated kuali with oil and deep fry Spring Roll until slightly brown.
3. Remove from oil and drain.
4. To serve, garnish with fried sliced onions and top with chilli sauce and black prawn paste.

Note:
Use small Po Piah Skin for this version.

PO PIAH: The true local crepe stuffed with stewed yambean and choice ingredients. One makes a side dish and two, a meal.

Acars

Vegetables, scalded and left to marinate in a choice blend of rempah, have been long part and parcel of nyonya culinary tradition. The test of a good nyonya cook was her ability to turn out an acar that was not only tempting but irresistable — a perfectly balanced combination of flavour, texture and colour. Understandably so, for a portion of acar entailed painstaking preparation and cooking. The rempah had to be blended and cooked to perfection, and the vegetables scalded to achieve the appealing texture and crispness after being sliced the right way. Choice fresh ingredients had to be used, including good vinegar. So important did the acar figure in a nyonya household that one made or broke one's reputation through it.

Usually served as a side dish, it can also be a one meal snack. The classic Penang Acar Awak is a good example of the latter, equally good eaten freshly cooked or when it had been cooled. Aside from fresh vegetables (long beans, cucumber, cauliflower, carrot, cabbage), salt fish, fruits (pineapple, mangoes), whole onions and garlic are also used for the pickled variety which is eaten as an appetizer or side dish at meal time.

The pickled variety could of course keep for months if stored in airtight jars and refrigerated after cooling. In the old days, acars were served in delicate small porcelain kum ching jars during festive occasions.

Top: ACAR AWAK No. 1
Top Right: ACAR NANAS
Below: ACAR LIMAU

GRIND (A), (B) AND (C) SEPARATELY TILL FINE:

(A) 3½ tbsp coriander (ketumbar)
     1 tsp fennel seeds (jintan manis)
     1 tsp cummin seeds (jintan putih)

(B) 10 dried chillies, soaked in warm water for 15 minutes
     for easier grinding.
     Thumb-sized piece fresh young turmeric (kunyit)

(C) 8 shallots
     5 pips garlic

PREPARATION

1. After removing the skin and eyes of the pineapple,
    remove the core. Cut into bitesize triangles.
2. Cut chillies into 1.5 cm lengths.

ACAR NANAS
(Pineapple Pickle)

Half a pineapple
3 cloves
2 star anise (bunga lawang)
2 pieces cinnamon sticks (kayu manis)
100 g sugar
3 fresh green chillies
Salt
2 stalks Indian curry leaves
17 tbsp cooking oil

PREPARATION

1. In heated frying pan, add oil.
2. When oil gets very hot, add C, stir for 1 minute.
3. Then add A and B plus cloves, star anise and cinnamon
    sticks. Stir well until fragrant.
4. Add pineapple slices, Indian curry leaves, sliced
    green chillies, salt and sugar to taste.
5. Reduce heat and stir until pineapple pieces are soft.
    Simmer for 1 hour. Serve.

Note:
No water is to be added during cooking. This will dilute the
taste.

ACAR LIMAU
(Lime Pickle)

300 g of half-ripe small limes

3½ tbsp coriander (ketumbar)	
40 fenugreek (halba)	(A)
1 tsp fennel seeds (jintan manis)	Ground finely
1 tsp poppy seeds (kas-kas)	
1 tsp cummin seeds (jintan putih)	

10 dried chillies, soaked in warm water	(B)
for 15 minutes	Ground finely
Thumbsized piece dried turmeric (kunyit)	

8 shallots	
4 pips garlic	pounded finely
4 tbsp vinegar	

3 cloves
2 star anise (bunga lawang)
5 cm cinnamon stick (kayu manis)
17 tbsp cooking oil
½ tsp salt
150 g sugar

PREPARATION

1. Clean limes and put in a bowl, add 2 tablespoonfuls salt and rub well into limes.
2. Season for 1 hour, then pour in hot water until it just covers the limes. Cover bowl and keep overnight.
3. Make cross shaped slits on top of the fruit. Slowly squeeze out the seeds with your fingers.
4. Spread on a plate and dry in the sun for 1 day.
5. Rub and stuff limes with sugar. Put them into a deep plate and cover well to prevent steam from entering. Steam for 15 minutes. Remove and cool.

METHOD

1. Heat a frying pan. Add oil. When oil is hot add pounded shallots and garlic. Stir for a minute.
2. Add ground ingredients (A) and (B), star anise, cloves and cinnamon stick. Stir until fragrant.
3. Add limes, vinegar, salt and sugar to taste.
4. Reduce heat and stir until limes are soft. Simmer for 1 hour.
5. Cool and store in pickling jars. Will keep for weeks if refrigerated.

Note:
No water is to be added when cooking. Sun the limes till completely dry.

From Top to Bottom: SALT FISH ACAR, ACAR BETIK, ACAR AWAK No. 2

ACAR AWAK (1)
(Mixed Vegetable Pickles)

1 cucumber
1 average-sized carrot
5 – 7 long beans
75 g cauliflower
3 – 5 french beans
75 g cabbage

2 fresh chillies
3.5 x 2.5 cm fresh young turmeric (kunyit)
2.5 cm square shrimp paste (belacan)
7 dried chillies
7 shallots
4 pips garlic

> Pounded finely

4 tbsp sugar
75 g finely pounded roasted groundnuts
9 – 10 tbsp cooking oil
½ tbsp salt

PREPARATION

1. Cut cucumber into quarters. Remove core, then cut into 3.5 centimetre pieces. Slice these lengthwise into two pieces each. Set aside.
2. Cut carrot as above.
3. Cut beans into 4 centimetre lengths.
4. Cut cauliflower into bite-size pieces.
5. Cut each french bean at a slant into three pieces.
6. Cut cabbage into bite-sized pieces.
7. Slice fresh red chillies into quarters lengthwise. Remove seeds.
8. Soak the dried chillies in warm water for 15 minutes.

METHOD

1. Heat a pot. Add about 2 rice bowls of water and bring to boil. Add 2 tablespoonfuls vinegar and ½ teaspoon salt.
2. Scald vegetables (one type at a time), for about half to 1 minute.
3. Remove, drain and pat dry with kitchen paper towels.
4. Heat a frying pan, add oil, then pounded ingredients. Stir until fragrant.
5. Next add in all the scalded vegetables, 2 tablespoonfuls vinegar, sugar and salt to taste.
6. Stir well for 1½ minutes until the gravy boils. Tip the mixture into a pot. Add in pounded roasted groundnuts. (You can also add two extra red chillies and 2 green chillies. Slice them into quarters lengthwise and remove seeds.)
7. Cover pot and simmer on low flame for about two hours. The longer you simmer it, the tastier the acar will be.
8. Cool, and store.

ACAR AWAK (2)
(Mixed Vegetable Acar)

If you prefer not to scald the vegetables first, give this other version of Acar Awak a try. You can vary the amount of vegetables according to how much of each type you prefer. The addition of sesame seeds depends very much on personal taste.

250 g long beans
200 g cabbage
200 g french beans
3 small or 2 medium-sized carrots
2 cucumbers
1 pineapple (optional)

30 dried chillies, soaked in warm water for 15 minutes
2 stalks lemon grass (serai)
4 cm piece galangal (lengkuas)
4 cm piece fresh young turmeric (kunyit)
4 cm piece shrimp paste (belacan)
6 candlenuts (buah keras)

> Ground finely

½ to ¾ rice bowl of finely pounded groundnuts
1 – 1½ tbsp sesame seeds
1 rice bowl of cooking oil
3 tbsp sugar
½ tbsp salt
2 tbsp vinegar

PREPARATION

1. Cut carrots into 1.2 cm lengths, quarter.
2. Cut cucumbers into quarters, remove core. Slice into 1.2 cm lengths and soak in a little salt water for half an hour Drain.
3. Skin pineapple, remove eyes and quarter, cut off core and cut into small bite-size triangles. Cut long beans, cabbage, french beans into bite-size pieces.

METHOD

1. Heat oil in kuali and fry ground ingredients until fragrant.
2. Add in sugar, salt and vinegar.
3. Add in vegetables, mixing well. Pour in pounded groundnuts.
4. Simmer the vegetables till cooked but still crispy. Sprinkle in sesame seeds.
5. Cool and store.

SALT FISH ACAR
(Salt Fish Pickle)

125 g salt fish flesh

3½ tbsp coriander (ketumbar)	
40 fenugreek (halba)	
½ tsp poppy seeds (kas-kas)	(A) Ground finely
1 tsp fennel seeds (jintan manis)	
1 tsp cummin seeds (jintan putih)	

10 dried chillies, soaked in warm water for 15 minutes for easy grinding	(B) Ground finely
Thumbsized piece turmeric (kunyit)	

8 shallots	Ground finely
4 pips garlic	

3 cloves
2 star anise (bunga lawang)
3 tbsp natural vinegar
150 g sugar
17 tbsp cooking oil
2 stalks Indian curry leaves

PREPARATION

1. Cut salt fish into small pieces (1.2 centimetre thick), soak in water for 15 minutes. Discard water, clean and drain.
2. Fry in oil until very light brown. Remove and set aside.

METHOD

1. Heat frying pan, add oil till hot. Add grounded shallots and garlic, stir for 1 minute, then add ground ingredients (A), cloves, star anise and (B).
2. Stir until fragrant, add salt fish, vinegar, Indian curry leaves, sugar and salt to taste. Reduce heat and stir for 2 minutes.
3. Reduce heat further and simmer for 1 hour.
4. Cool, store in a jar. It can be kept for many days without spoiling.

Note:
No water is to be added while cooking.

ACAR BETIK
(Papaya Pickle)

600 g near-ripe papaya
4 tbsp vinegar with 3 tbsp water
6½ tbsp sugar
1 tsp salt

PREPARATION

1. Skin papaya, discard the part nearest stem. Cut into quarters.
2. Remove seeds and a thin layer of inner part.
3. Slice finely. Wash and drain in metal sieve.

METHOD

1. Put the cut papaya into a porcelain or pickle jar, add vinegar, sugar and salt. Mix well. Cover and keep overnight. Serve.

Note:
This pickle will keep indefinitely if refrigerated.

PURUT IKAN

300 g small prawns, shelled, washed and drained
½ pineapple
2 long brinjals
115 g long beans
115 g cabbage, shredded
2 bunches of laksa leaves (daun kesom)
2 bunches daun kaduk
1 bunch mint leaves (daun pudina)
1 phaeomaria (bunga kantan), cut into half, shredded
1 small red carrot
1 stalk lemon grass (serai), sliced finely
3 – 4 daun limau purut
5 dried chillies, soaked in warm water for 15 minutes
4 fresh red chillies, cut into small slices
10 shallots, skinned, cut into small pieces
2 tamarind pieces (assam keping)
1 big bottle of purut ikan
1 tbsp sugar
1 tomato, cut into 8 pieces
4½ rice bowls of water
1 tbsp shrimp paste (belacan)

PREPARATION

1. Skin pineapple, remove the eyes and slice into bite-size pieces.
2. Place 3 to 4 daun kaduk leaves on top of each other, wrap some mint, daun limau purut and laksa leaves together, then shred. Repeat with all the daun kaduk leaves.
3. Pound chillies and serai finely. Add shallots and pound fairly fine.
4. Wash all vegetables and cut into 5 centimetre lengths.
5. Open the bottle of purut ikan, wash well, drain.

PURUT IKAN: This recipe elevates the usually discarded portion of fishes to the main ingredient of a tasty soupy salad. Bottled ikan purut is very fishy and must be washed thoroughly before use.

METHOD

1. Put 4½ rice bowls water in a pot. Add ground ingredients, tamarind pieces and shrimp paste, dissolve shrimp paste with a spoon.
2. Heat pot and bring to boil, add carrot and long beans. Lower heat to medium and boil for 5 minutes, add prawns and brinjals. Boil until soft.
3. Add phaeomaria, pineapple, purut ikan, tomato slices, ½ teaspoon salt and 1 tablespoonful sugar. Adjust to personal taste. Boil until all ingredients are soft.
4. Lower heat and simmer for ½ an hour and serve.

MANGO ACAR: A spicy pickle that will whet any appitite. Taste raw mango before preparing spices. If they are too sour, go easy on the vinegar and add more sugar.

ACAR KUNYIT IKAN
(Fish Pickle)

'Acar kunyit ikan' was the one dish that had star status at nyonya wedding feasts. On such festive occasions, tables brimmed with scores of dishes which took master chefs or 'chong phohs' days to prepare.

10 hardtails (ikan cencaru)
200 – 300 g young ginger
80 – 100 g garlic
3 fresh green chillies
3 fresh red chillies
3 cm fresh young turmeric (kunyit), pounded finely
18 tbsp cooking oil
10 tbsp local vinegar
1 tsp salt
5 tbsp sugar

PREPARATION

1. Remove scales, gills and intestines of fish. Leave heads intact. Clean fish, and season with 1½ teaspoonfuls salt for 15 minutes. Then fry until light brown, remove and place on a plate.
2. Skin ginger. Shred. Place on a plate spreading it out well. Dry in the sun for 15 minutes. Then fry until light brown, remove.
3. Slice garlic into thin pieces, fry until light brown and put with fried ginger.
4. Slice green and red chillies into quarters and remove seeds. Lower heat after frying garlic. Into the same oil, add chillies and stir for a few seconds. Remove quickly into the same plate as the fried ginger and garlic.

METHOD

1. Heat a kuali. Add cooking oil. When oil is hot, fry pounded turmeric, then reduce heat slightly. Stir slowly until the oil becomes yellow. Add vinegar and stir further.
2. Reduce heat to low and remove turmeric residue with a handled metal sieve. Into the same oil, add sugar and salt and stir slowly until sugar dissolves.
3. Turn off heat. Into a clean and dry glass bowl or porcelain pot (do not use aluminium pot) place half of the fish to form a first layer. Use half of the fried ginger, garlic and chillies as a second layer. Then add the remaining half of the fish as a third layer and the rest of the fried ingredients as the fourth. Pour in the yellow oil, vinegar and sugar. Cover bowl or pot for a few hours. The longer the fish is soaked, the tastier it will turn out. This pickle can keep for several days with refrigeration.

MANGO ACAR
(Mango Pickle)

300 g young mango

3½ tbsp coriander (ketumbar)	
40 fenugreek (halba)	
1 tsp fennel seeds (jintan manis)	(A) Ground finely
½ tsp poppy seeds (kas-kas)	
1 tsp cummin seeds (jintan putih)	

10 dried chillies, soaked in warm water for 15 minutes for easy grinding	(B) Ground finely
3.5 cm turmeric (kunyit)	

8 shallots	Ground finely
4 pips garlic	

19 tbsp cooking oil
1 small piece ginger, skinned, sliced finely
2½ tbsp vinegar
½ tsp salt
Sugar to taste — about 150 g
3 cloves
5 cm cinnamon sticks (kayu manis)
2 star anise (bunga lawang)
A few stalks Indian curry leaves.

PREPARATION

1. Cut mangoes into quarters, remove seeds, wash and drain.
2. Rub 3 tablespoonfuls salt into mangoes and season for 36 hours. Wash away all the salt and cut mangoes into 3 pieces each. Do not use old mangoes because they are fibrous and hard.

METHOD

1. Heat frying pan, add oil. When oil is hot, add the ground onions and garlic. Stir for 1 minute, then add star anise, cloves, cinnamon sticks, ginger and ground ingredients (A). Then add (B).
2. Stir until fragrant, add mangoes, vinegar, Indian curry leaves, salt and sugar to taste.
3. Reduce to low heat and cook until mangoes are soft.
4. Remove heat and let stand for 1 hour.

Note:
1. Grinding of shallots and garlic and ingredients (A) should be done separately.
2. Amount of sugar should be adjusted to suit individual taste.
3. No water is to be added while cooking.

Gulais

Gulai is the nyonya term for curry. A nyonya gulai has a flavour and bite that is distinctively its own.

The combination of ingredients create a mind-boggling aromatic tapestry. In most recipes, more than liberal use of coconut milk, lemon grass, turmeric, prawn paste, fennel seeds, cummin seeds, tamarind as well as fresh and dry chillies contribute to this. The result: a curry that is rich, hot, aromatic, and tangy all at the same time; a perfect blend that is exquisitely combined, yet subtle in flavour. This is the rare distinction of a nyonya gulai where overpoweringly pungent ingredients are blended into a harmonious delight.

The variety of gulais from a nyonya kitchen is extraordinary, the main ingredients ranging from nangka (jackfruit) to pineapple and sweet potato leaves to salt fish.

Whether sour-hot, sweet and tangy or heavily spiced, a nyonya gulai is always delicious.

GULAI LEMAK NANAS
(Pineapple Curry With Prawns)

300 g medium-sized prawns
½ coconut, grated
3 tbsp coriander (ketumbar)
1 stalk lemon grass (serai)
5 shallots
3 pips garlic
3.5 cm fresh young turmeric (kunyit)
5 dried chillies
4 fresh red chillies
½ tsp shrimp paste (belacan)
1 small pineapple
8 tbsp cooking oil
Salt to taste

PREPARATION

1. Shell prawns, wash, drain and pat dry with kitchen paper towels.
2. Add one rice bowl of water to coconut and squeeze for first milk. Add another 2 rice bowls of water to coconut and squeeze for second milk. Set aside.
3. Soak dried chillies in warm water for 15 minutes to make for easier grinding.
4. Skin pineapple, remove the eyes, wash and cut into quarters. Remove core, then cut into small triangular pieces.

METHOD

1. Grind coriander into a fine paste. Do the same for all the cut ingredients (ie. serai, chillies, turmeric, shallots and garlic.)
2. Heat a pot, pour in oil. Add in ground ingredients after oil is hot. Stir for a minute before adding coriander and shrimp paste.
3. For easy stirring, add second coconut milk bit by bit. This also prevents burning.
4. When mixture starts to bubble, add prawns. Stir for a minute, add in the rest of second coconut milk. Add pineapple and salt to taste.
5. Boil till pineapple is soft. Add first coconut milk and continue cooking for a few minutes.
6. Lower heat, cover pot and simmer for 20 – 30 minutes before serving.

Note:
Each spice has to be ground finely before the next is added and ground.

GULAI LEMAK NANAS: Fresh prawns, a favourite ingredient in northern nyonya kitchens are stewed in a curry with pineapple. The tangy fruit counteracts cloyness and makes the dish one which is simply irresistable.

GULAI NASI KUNYIT

1 kg chicken

4 tbsp coriander (ketumbar)	(A)
1 tsp cummin seeds (jintan putih)	Ground finely

1 stalk lemon grass (serai)	(B)
Thumbsized piece fresh turmeric (kunyit)	Ground finely
10 dried chillies	

10 shallots
4 pips garlic
¾ coconut, grated
2 star anise (bunga lawang)
3 cloves (bunga cengkih)
2 thumbsized pieces cinnamon sticks (kayu manis)
Salt to taste

PREPARATION

1. Clean and cut chicken to pieces.
2. Grind (A) finely, set aside.
3. Soak chillies in warm water for 15 minutes. Grind (B) finely.
4. Pound shallots and garlic finely.
5. Add 3 bowls of water to grated coconut to squeeze for milk. Set aside.

METHOD

1. Heat pan, add 9 tablespoonfuls cooking oil. When oil is hot, add all the ground and pounded ingredients. Stir until fragrant.
2. Add a few tablespoonfuls coconut milk to keep the mixture in the pot wet. Stir for 1 minute, add chicken pieces.
3. Stir well, add a few more tablespoonfuls coconut milk and stir again for 2 to 3 minutes.
4. Pour in the rest of the coconut milk till the chicken is covered add star anise, cloves, cinnamon sticks and salt to taste.
5. Slow boil until chicken is cooked. Lower heat and simmer for 1 hour.
6. Serve with nasi kunyit (see page 106).

GULAI NASI KUNYIT: The illustration shows both the curry and the nasi kunyit served in their traditional containers. The Indian clay pot or belanga brings out the best in any curry.

BITTERGOURD GULAI
(Bittergourd Curry)

300 g pork (more lean than fat)
300 g prawns
¾ coconut, grated
3 heaped tbsp coriander (ketumbar)
1 tsp cummin seeds (jintan putih)
5 dried chillies, soaked in warm water for 15 minutes
3 fresh red chillies
6 shallots
3 pips garlic
14 fried soya bean cakes (taupok)
1 big bittergourd
2.5 piece fresh turmeric (kunyit)
11 tbsp cooking oil
Salt to taste
1 tbsp light soya sauce
1 tbsp pepper

PREPARATION

1. Mince pork.
2. Shell, wash and drain prawns. Mince.
3. Cut bittergourd into slices (2.5 cm thick) at a slant.
4. Grind coriander, cummin seeds and turmeric finely.
5. Grind chillies finely.
6. Pound or grind shallots and garlic finely.
7. Add 1 rice bowl of water to coconut and squeeze for first milk.
8. Add 3 rice bowls of water to the same grated coconut and squeeze for second milk.
9. Cut fried soya bean cake into halves.

METHOD

1. Put minced pork and prawns into a bowl, add 2 tablespoonful light soya sauce, 1 tablespoonful pepper, stir to mix well.
2. Stuff the mixture into the cut bittergourd.
3. Heat pot, add oil till hot, add ground shallots, chillies and garlic, stir for a few seconds then add ground coriander, cummin seeds and turmeric. Stir and add a few tablespoonfuls second coconut milk until fragrant.
4. Add remaining second coconut milk and cook until gravy is fairly thick, then add stuffed bittergourd, pieces of fried soya bean cake and salt to taste. Slow boil for another few minutes. Lower heat and simmer for ½ an hour. Serve.

GULAI LEMAK KEPALA IKAN KERING
(Dried Fish Head Curry Lemak)

½ dried fish head

1 tbsp cummin seeds (jintan puteh)	
4 tbsp coriander (ketumbar)	
9 shallots	
¾ tbsp fennel seeds (jintan manis)	
3 pips garlic	(A)
3.5 cm fresh young turmeric (kunyit)	Ground finely
1 small stalk lemon grass (serai)	
9 dried chillies	
2.5 cm shrimp paste (belacan)	

¾ coconut, grated
250 g long beans
2 brinjals
300 g prawns
10 tbsp cooking oil
Salt to taste

PREPARATION

1. Shell prawns, wash and drain.
2. Soak dried chillies in warm water for 15 minutes.
3. Add a rice bowl of water to grated coconut and squeeze for the first milk. Add another 3 bowls of water to the same grated coconut and squeeze for second milk. Set aside.
4. Cut brinjals into 5 centimetre long pieces, then slit into quarters.
5. Grind (A) finely.
6. Cut fish head into pieces and soak in water for ½ hour.

METHOD

1. Heat oil in cooking pot. Reduce heat to medium. Add ground ingredients and belacan. Stir for a minute.
2. Add first coconut milk little by little until mixture is fragrant. Stir well to prevent mixture in the pot from burning.
3. Add dried fish head and prawns. Stir for a minute before adding second coconut milk.
4. If gravy is too thick, add a little water to grated coconut and squeeze for third milk. Then add milk little by little till desired consistency of gravy is achieved.
5. Add long beans and brinjals, bring to boil until all ingredients are cooked.
6. Lower heat and simmer for 20 – 30 minutes. Serve.

GULAI LEMAK BRINJALS OR LONG BEANS

(Rich Brinjal or Long Bean Curry)

300 g brinjals or long beans
75 g dried prawns or 200 g medium-sized prawns
½ coconut, grated

5 shallots
3 pips garlic   Pounded fairly fine
Thumb-sized pieces fresh
    young turmeric (kunyit)

3 fresh red chillies, pounded finely
1 tsp shrimp paste
Salt to taste
5 tbsp cooking oil

PREPARATION

1. Discard stalks of brinjals. Slice into two lengthwise. Then cut into 5 centimetre slices. Wash and drain.
2. Cut off the two ends of long beans then slice into 5 centimetre lengths. Wash and drain.
3. Add ½ a rice bowl of water to the grated coconut and squeeze for first milk. Then add another 5 rice bowls water to the same coconut and squeeze for second milk.
4. Shell prawns and discard heads. Wash and drain.
5. Pound the shallots, turmeric and chillies fairly fine.

METHOD

1. Heat oil in pot. Add pounded ingredients, shrimp paste and dried prawns. Stir for 1 minute.
2. Pour in coconut milk. Add brinjals or long beans. Bring to slow boil until vegetables are soft and cooked.
3. Add salt to taste. Serve.

Note:
If you want a less thick gravy, squeeze for third coconut milk and add.

GULAI NANGKA

(Jackfruit Curry)

450 g young jackfruit (nangka)
150 g dried prawns
8 shallots
4 fresh red chillies
Thumbsized piece fresh turmeric (kunyit)
1 stalk lemon grass (serai)
1 coconut, grated
Salt to taste
3 cm x 5 cm piece shrimp paste (belacan)
Monosodium glutamate/seasoning (optional)

PREPARATION

1. Remove skin of jackfruit using pith and pulp with seeds intact. Cut into bite-sized pieces. Boil till half cooked. Dish out. Set aside.
2. Wash, drain the dried prawns. Set aside.
3. Slice lemon grass finely and pound. Add chillies and turmeric and pound finely. Then add shallots and pound finely. Dish out into a bowl.
4. Add 1 rice bowl of water to grated coconut and squeeze for first milk.
5. Add another 2 rice bowls of water to the same grated coconut and squeeze for second milk.

METHOD

1. Fill pot with the second coconut milk, dried prawns, pounded ingredients, shrimp paste and half cooked jackfruit. Bring to boil until jackfruit is fully cooked and soft. Add the first santan, pinch of seasoning and salt to taste. Boil for another 2 to 3 minutes. Adjust to low. Simmer a while. Serve.

Note:
Rub the jackfruit with a little oil as it is cut to prevent sap from oozing out.

(OVERLEAF) GULAI NANGKA: A rich curry using very young jackfruit. Note that the pulp of the fruit is barely developed and the seed is, therefore, soft enough to be eaten.

GULAI LEMAK BRINJALS: A recipe with many variations. Choose among the different types of brinjals, long beans and fresh or dried prawns.

GULAI SALT FISH PINEAPPLE
(Salt Fish Pineapple Curry)

600 g salt fish
½ kg cockles (kerang)
1 long brinjal
150 g long beans
1 small ripe pineapple
½ coconut, grated

1 stalk lemon grass (serai)
6 dried chillies, soaked in warm water
    for 15 minutes   (A)
3 fresh red chillies
3.5 cm fresh turmeric (kunyit)
9 shallots
3 pips garlic

6 tbsp coriander (ketumbar)
1 tsp fennel seeds (jintan manis)
1 tsp cummin seeds (jintan putih)   (B)

8 tbsp cooking oil
Salt

PREPARATION

1. Soak salt fish head or bones in water for 10 minutes.
2. Wash cockles and soak in boiling water for 1 minute. Drain and shell.
3. Skin pineapple, clean and quarter, remove core and cut into triangular pieces.
4. Cut brinjal into half, then into 3.5 cm pieces.
5. Cut long beans into 3.5 cm pieces.
6. Add 1½ rice bowls of water to the grated coconut to squeeze for first milk.
7. Add another 4½ rice bowls of water to the coconut and squeeze for second milk.
8. Grind (A) finely. Set aside.
9. Grind (B) finely. Set aside.

METHOD

1. Heat pot, add oil. When oil is hot, add (A). Stir for 1 minute, then add rempah (B).
2. Reduce heat and stir well until fragrant. The mixture should be bubbling in oil. If it has dried up add a little more oil.
3. Skim the top of the second coconut milk and add to the mixture, stir well for ½ minute before adding the rest of the second coconut milk.
4. Add salt fish head or bones, pineapple and long beans. Bring up heat. Boil for 2½ minutes, then add brinjals.
5. When brinjals start to get soft reduce heat and cover pot to simmer for ½ hour. Add cockles before serving.

Notes:

1. If the salt fish head or bones are not soaked in water the curry may become too saltish.
2. While stirring the mixture in the pot reduce heat as a metal pot gets hot very fast. Care has to be taken or the gravy will get burnt.
3. A fairly ripe pineapple (but not over ripe) will add natural sweetness to the curry.
4. This delicious curry if well-cooked should be just oily, with a red and yellowish colouring. If it is too yellowish it means too much turmeric has been used and the dish will not taste right.

JANTUNG PISANG GULAI LEMAK
(Rich Banana Bud Curry)

300 g banana bud centres (jantung pisang)
½ coconut, grated
225 g fresh prawns
3 shallots
1 tsp pounded chilli
1 tsp shrimp paste (belacan)
Salt and pepper to taste

PREPARATION

1. Peel banana bud removing all layers of purple skin and yellow flowers till you see the pinkish-white heart of the bud. Cut this into four and boil in 2 rice bowls of water for 2 – 3 minutes until it is half-cooked.
2. Remove banana bud centres and slice at a slant into bitesize pieces. Set aside.
3. Squeeze 1 rice bowl of first milk from grated coconut. Add another rice bowl and squeeze for second milk.
4. Peel, wash and drain prawns.
5. Slice shallots and pound with shrimp paste.

METHOD

1. Put second milk into pot and add pounded chilli, onions, shrimp paste and prawns.
2. When mixture boils and prawns are nearly cooked, add banana bud centres and salt and pepper to taste. Let it boil for a few minutes until fragrant.
3. Add first coconut milk and remove quickly when this boils.

Note:
You can substitute 50 g of anchovies or dried prawns for fresh prawns in this dish.

PORK GULAI NYONYA STYLE
(Pork Curry Nyonya Style)

450 g lean pork with a little fat
300 g potato (preferably yellow)
1 stalk lemon grass (serai)

6 shallots
4 pips garlic   (A)

3.5 cm turmeric (kunyit)
7 dried chillies, soaked in warm water
   for 15 minutes   (B)
3 fresh red chillies
4 tbsp coriander (ketumbar)
1 tsp fennel seeds (jintan manis)

½ coconut, grated
1 star anise (bunga lawang)
3 cloves (bunga cengkih)
1 cinnamon stick (kayu manis)
11 tbsp cooking oil

PREPARATION

1. Cut pork into bitesize pieces, wash and drain.
2. Skin potatoes and cut into 4 pieces at a slant, soak in water and drain.
3. Grind (A) finely, set aside. Grind (B) finely, set aside.
4. Add 1½ rice bowls water to grated coconut to squeeze for first milk. Set aside.
5. Add again 2 rice bowls of water to the same grated coconut and squeeze for second milk. Set aside.

METHOD

1. Heat pot, add oil. When hot, add (A), stir for 1 minute, then add (B). Then add cloves and cinnamon stick, reduce heat slightly or mixture will burn.
2. Stir until fragrant. While stirring, keep the mixture wet by adding a little of the second santan.
3. Add pork, stir for 1 minute, add a little second coconut milk or oil if it is too dry.
4. Pour in all the remaining second coconut milk, add potatoes and salt to taste.
5. Cover pot and slow boil until potatoes and pork are cooked. Add the first coconut milk and boil again for a few minutes. Lower heat and simmer for ½ an hour. Serve.

Note:
Do not discard the grated coconut. If gravy is insufficient add some water and squeeze for a third milk, dilute accordingly.

GULAI IKAN NYONYA STYLE
(Fish Curry Nyonya Style)

300 g fillet of fish or whole fish
½ coconut, grated

3 heaped tbsp coriander (ketumbar)
1 tsp fennel seeds (jintan manis)   (A)

1 stalk lemon grass (serai) cleaned and
   cut into small pieces
Thumbsized piece fresh turmeric,
   skinned and cleaned   (B)
5 dried chillies
4 fresh red chillies, sliced finely

1 tomato, cut into 8 pieces
8 tbsp cooking oil

PREPARATION

1. Discard scales, gills and intestines of fish. Clean fish and drain.
2. Rub a little salt on the fish and season for 10 to 15 minutes.
3. Soak dried chillies in warm water for 15 minutes, this is for easy grinding.
4. Grind (A) finely. Set aside.
5. Then grind (B) till fine. If the ingredients are too dry after grinding sprinkle a little water to make it a thick paste. Be careful not to add too much water.
6. Add 1½ ricebowls water to grated coconut to squeeze for first milk. Set aside.
7. Add another 2 rice bowls water to the same grated coconut to squeeze for second milk. Set aside. Do not throw away the grated coconut. If a thinner gravy is required, add water and squeeze for a third milk.

METHOD

1. Heat pot, add cooking oil. When hot add all the ground ingredients and stir well for 1¼ minutes, reduce to medium heat to prevent mixture from burning.
2. Skim the top of the second coconut milk, add to the mixture and stir till fragrant. The ingredients should be bubbling in oil by now. If this is not so, add a little oil.
3. Pour in the remaining second coconut milk, add fish, bring up heat to boil.
4. When fish is about to cook, add the first coconut milk, tomato slices and salt to taste.
5. When fish is cooked, lower heat, cover pot and simmer for ½ an hour. Serve hot.

CRAB GULAI
(Crab Curry)

1 kg land crab
½ coconut, grated

3 tbsp coriander (ketumbar)
1 tsp cummin seeds (jintan putih)
½ tsp fennel seeds (jintan manis)   (A)
¼ tsp fenugreek (halba)
¼ tsp poppy seeds (kas-kas)

8 dried chillies, soaked for 15 minutes
2.5 cm fresh turmeric (kunyit)
6 shallots   (B)
4 pips garlic

Some Indian curry leaves
9 tbsp oil

PREPARATION

---

1. Shell crab and remove unwanted parts. Wash, drain and cut into quarters.
2. Grind (A) finely. Set aside.
3. Grind (B) finely. Set aside.
4. Add 1½ rice bowls of water to grated coconut and squeeze for milk.

METHOD

---

1. Heat pot, add 9 tablespoonfuls of oil hot. Add (B) stir for ½ a minute then add (A). Fry until fragrant adding some coconut milk to wet the ingredients while stirring.
2. Add crabs, stir for a few minutes and cover. When crab is half cooked, add curry leaves and 1 teaspoonful of salt and all the coconut milk. Cover, stirring often until crab is reddish and cooked.
3. Remove heat when gravy starts to thicken. Dish out and serve.

GULAI TUMIS KEPALA IKAN
(Fish Head Curry)

1 medium-sized fish head. Use either threadfin (kurau), spanish mackerel (tenggiri) or red snapper (merah)

8 dried chillies
10 shallots
1 stalk lemon grass (serai) cut into   (A)
   small pieces   ground finely
3 pips garlic
Thumbsized piece fresh
   young turmeric (kunyit)

One 2.5 cm square piece shrimp paste (belacan)
1½ pieces tamarind (assam keping)
3 stalks polygonum (daun kesum)
1 phaeomaria (bunga kantan)
11 tbsp cooking oil
3½ rice bowls of water
Salt to taste

PREPARATION

---

1. Wash, drain fish head.
2. Remove polygonum stalks. Wash and drain leaves.
3. Grind (A) finely.

METHOD

---

1. Heat pot and add cooking oil. When oil is hot, reduce heat and add ground ingredients and belacan. Stir until fragrant.
2. Add polygonum, phaeomaria and fish head. Stir for 1 minute.
3. Add water, tamarind pieces and salt to taste. Increase heat and boil until fish head is cooked.
4. Lower heat, cover pot and simmer. Serve.

GULAI TUMIS KEPALA IKAN: A simple curry, but good enough to impress any guest. Choose a fish head with a good portion of flesh.

GULAI AYAM

1 chicken of about 1 kg in weight
4 tbsp coriander (ketumbar)
1 tbsp cummin seeds (jintan putih)
2.5 cm fresh turmeric (kunyit)
Thumbsized piece fresh young ginger
10 shallots
5 pips garlic
10 dried chillies, soaked in warm water for 15 minutes
1 coconut, grated
1 stalk lemon grass (serai)
300 g potatoes
12 tbsp cooking oil

PREPARATION

1. Clean chicken, drain. Cut into required pieces.
2. Grind coriander and cummin seeds finely.
3. Grind lemon grass and chillies finely.
4. Grind shallots, garlic and ginger finely.
5. Add 3½ rice bowls of water to grated coconut to squeeze for milk.
6. Boil potatoes after cleaning. When three quarters cooked, peel off skin and cut into halves.

METHOD

1. Put 12 tablespoonfuls oil into a heated pot. When oil is hot, add all the ground ingredients. Stir until fragrant. Add some coconut milk while stirring to prevent gravy getting burnt.
2. Add chicken pieces, stir, then add the rest of the coconut milk.
3. Simmer, when chicken pieces are about to cook, add the potatoes, and salt to taste.
4. Continue simmering till the potatoes are fully cooked. Serve.

Sambals

Sambal belacan, a pounded mixture of two ingredients (chillies and belacan) is seldom missing from a nyonya meal. Fiery and fragrant (or pungent, depending on how your nostrils take it) with a slight sharp sour tang — this from the juice of the limau kasturi (small limes) squeezed in for good measure — it is a complement that goes with any and every dish.

When combined with any number of fresh vegetables or fried ingredients, it becomes an instant and convenient one dish meal.

Nyonya cooks prepare their sambals the traditional way — using the lesong (mortar and pestle). According to a relative (well known for her lip smacking, tasty sambals) chillies should go into the lesong first and the toasted belacan should be added to the chillies and pounded into them when it is still hot. This way, the chillies will absorb the belacan taste and give that distinctive fragrance and sharp smack that a cold piece of belacan ground with chillies in a blender cannot produce.

And if you include heh bee (dried prawns), soak them for a couple of minutes in a little water till they just bloat. Drain the dried prawns well, then pound them in the lesong after removing the pounded sambal belacan.

For those who prefer a raw, searing chilli taste in their mouth, pound chillies and belacan a couple of times only until the chillies break. Then remove to a dish.

SAMBAL GORENG UDANG
(Fried Prawn Sambal)

300 g medium-sized prawns
½ medium-sized coconut, grated
4 pips garlic
2 stalks lemon grass (serai)
2 shallots
2 green chillies
1 tomato
1 medium-sized tamarind piece (assam keping)
8 cashew nuts
10 tbsp cooking oil
Salt to taste

PREPARATION

1. Shell prawns. Wash and drain.
2. Slice garlic thinly.
3. Slice lemon grass into small pieces and pound finely.
4. Cut chillies into quarters and remove seeds.
5. Cut tomato into eights.
6. Add ½ rice bowl of water to grated coconut. Squeeze out first milk into a bowl. Set aside. Add another ¾ to 1 cup of water to grated coconut. Squeeze for second milk. Set aside.
7. Slice shallots. Fry until transparent and set aside.

METHOD

1. Heat a frying pan. Add cooking oil. Fry garlic and pounded lemon grass. Stir these two ingredients until they turn light brown.
2. Reduce heat, add prawns and cashew nuts together with first coconut milk. Stir until prawns are three quarters cooked.
3. Add second coconut milk, green chillies, tamarind piece, cut tomato and salt to taste.
4. Allow to boil for a few minutes before turning off heat.
5. Garnish with fried shallots. Serve.

SAMBAL GORENG UDANG: Not many spices are used in this unusual sambal but the distinctive nutty flavour of this dish makes it a favourite among the whole family.

MANGO SAMBAL

4 small young mangoes
4 fresh red chillies
2 tbsp shrimp paste (belacan)
Sugar to taste (about 2 tbsp)

PREPARATION

1. Skin mango, clean, cut into half and remove seeds. Cut into bite-sized pieces.
2. Pound chillies finely.
3. Toast shrimp paste after pressing into a thin wafer. Alternately, heat in frying pan till crumbly and fragrant. Add shrimp paste to pounded chillies and pound again till both are well mixed.

METHOD

1. Place mangoes into a bowl. Add pounded ingredients. Stir to mix and ensure that the mango pieces are well coated with the pounded mixture. If it is only for a single serving, use just sufficient mango slices and the required amount of pounded mixture.
2. A teaspoonful of thick dark sauce and light soya sauce may be added according to individual taste.

GREEN CHILLI SAMBAL

600 g green chillies
A handful of anchovies (ikan bilis)

2 big onions
3 candlenuts (buah keras)   Pounded finely

3 – 4 tbsp cooking oil
1 grated coconut, add 2½ rice bowls of water to squeeze for milk

METHOD

1. Slice chillies into 1½ – 2 centimetre lengths.
2. Heat oil in kuali. Fry anchovies till crisp. Set aside.
3. In same oil, fry pounded onions and candlenuts, then add sliced chillies and salt to taste.
4. Add coconut milk and anchovies. Quick stir for a couple of minutes and simmer till dry and oil begins to surface.
5. Remove and serve with rice.

SAMBAL UDANG GORENG ASSAM
(Prawns in Tamarind Sambal)

600 g fairly big prawns

5 dried chillies	
3 fresh red chillies	
6 shallots	Pounded finely
4 pips garlic	
1½ tbsp shrimp paste (belacan)	

½ tsp thick dark soya sauce
2 tsp tamarind pulp (assam jawa)
1 tbsp sugar
¼ tsp salt
½ tsp pepper
9 tbsp cooking oil

PREPARATION

1. Clip off tips of heads and tails of prawns. Remove veins of prawns by cutting through the shells. Drain. Dry with kitchen paper towels.
2. Put tamarind paste into a bowl. Add a teaspoonful or two of water. Dissolve with fingers and strain.
3. Add the strained liquid to thick dark soya sauce.

METHOD

1. Pound fresh and dried chillies, shallots, garlic and shrimp paste.
2. Add mixture of tamarind juice, thick dark soya sauce, sugar, pepper and salt to prawns. Rub in well, season for ½ hour.
3. Heat frying pan. Add oil and fry pounded ingredients till fragrant. Put in prawns and stir well.
4. Control heat so prawns get cooked without being burnt. Serve.

Note:

The seasoning mixture for the prawns must be of a thick consistency if this dish is to taste good. Too thin a paste will result in a tasteless dish.

SAMBAL TUMIS KERANG
(Fried Cockles in Sambal)

900 g cockles (kerang)
6 dried chillies
3 fresh red chillies
6 shallots
3 pips garlic
1 stalk lemon grass (serai)
½ tsp shrimp paste (belacan)
½ tsp sugar
1 tbsp tamarind paste (assam jawa)
11 tbsp cooking oil
Salt to taste

PREPARATION

1. Clean, drain and put cockles into container. Pour boiling water until it covers cockles, after 5 minutes, discard water and shell. Put into a colander and wash away remaining blood.
2. Soak dried chillies in warm water for 15 minutes.
3. Pound dried chillies with red chillies finely.
4. Slice shallots and garlic. Add to pounded fresh and dried chillies and pound again till fairly fine.
5. Bruise lemon grass.
6. Dissolve tamarind paste in ½ rice bowl of water.

METHOD

1. Heat frying pan. Add oil.
2. Add pounded ingredients, lemon grass and shrimp paste. Stir until fragrant.
3. Add tamarind juice, sugar and salt to taste.
4. When gravy is boiling, add cockles, stir for ½ to 1 minute. Serve.

Note:

If cockles are not rinsed well of blood, the gravy will turn blackish. Cockles should not be boiled too long; they will shrink and become tough.

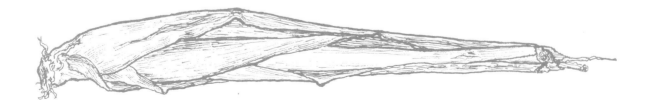

SAMBAL IKAN BILIS
(Anchovy Sambal)

150 g fresh anchovy (ikan bilis basah)
1 stalk lemon grass (serai)
5 dried chillies
3 fresh red chillies
3.5 cm fresh young turmeric (kunyit)
8 shallots
3 pips garlic
1 tsp shrimp paste (belacan)
1 tsp tamarind paste (assam jawa)
Thumb-sized piece of ginger
10 tbsp cooking oil
Salt to taste.

PREPARATION

1. Discard anchovy heads and stomachs. Clean, drain.
2. Cut lemon grass into slices. Discard end.
3. Soak dried chillies in warm water for 15 minutes.
4. Pound lemon grass, fresh and dried chillies finely.
5. Skin turmeric then add to above pounded ingredients and pound again.
6. Slice shallots and garlic. Add to above pounded ingredients and pound till nearly fine.
7. Dissolve tamarind paste in 1 cup water. Remove seeds, strain for liquid.
8. Shred ginger.

METHOD

1. Add oil to heated frying pan.
2. Add pounded ingredients, shredded ginger and shrimp paste. Stir till fragrant.
3. Add anchovies stir fry for a minute and add a little of the tamarind juice.
4. Stir for 1 minute and add some of the remaining tamarind juice till gravy is quite thick. Taste for sourness.
5. Add sugar and salt to taste.
6. Stir for a few minutes. Serve.

SAMBAL HEH BEE
(Dried Prawn Sambal)

300 g dried prawns
8 shallots
4 pips garlic
9 dried chillies
3 cm fresh young turmeric (kunyit)
1 stalk lemon grass (serai)
1 tsp shrimp paste (belacan)
1 tbsp tamarind paste (assam jawa)
2½ tbsp sugar
3 young daun limau purut
14 tbsp cooking oil
Salt to taste

PREPARATION

1. Discard heads and shells of prawns. Soak in water for 5 minutes. Drain, dry and pound coarsely.
2. Slice shallots and garlic.
3. Soak dried chillies in warm water for 10 – 15 minutes. Remove and pound with kunyit.
4. After pounding dried chillies and turmeric finely, add shallots and garlic and pound again till fairly fine.
5. Cut lemon grass into two and bruise.
6. Dissolve tamarind paste in ½ rice bowl of water. Discard seeds and strain. Keep aside.
7. Shred daun limau purut.

METHOD

1. Heat frying pan. Add oil.
2. Add pounded ingredients, shrimp paste and lemon grass. Stir until fragrant. Control heat to prevent burning.
3. Add pounded dried prawns and half of the tamarind juice. Stir for 2 minutes.
4. Add the rest of the tamarind juice, sugar, daun limau purut and salt to taste.
5. Stir until dish is cooked to your taste; either with gravy or almost dry. Serve.

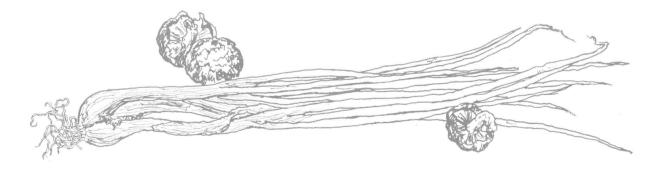

SAMBAL IKAN SUMBAT
(Stuffed Fish Sambal)

450 g black pomfret (bawal hitam)

5 shallots
2 pips garlic
4 fresh red chillies
1 stalk lemon grass (serai) sliced   (A)
   into small pieces
Thumb-sized piece shrimp paste (belacan)
2 cm fresh young turmeric (kunyit)

1 tsp tamarind paste (assam jawa)
2 daun limau purut, shredded
1 tsp sugar
Cooking oil
Salt to taste

PREPARATION

1. Remove gills and intestines of fish. Clean. Slit both sides of fish horizontally without cutting through. Rub a little salt on the fish and season for a while.
2. Add 3 tablespoons water to tamarind and squeeze for juice. Put the mixture through a sieve and discard the pulp and seeds. Set juice aside.
3. Pound (A) coarsely.

METHOD

1. Mix pounded ingredients, daun limau purut, sugar and a little salt with tamarind juice.
2. Stuff the two slits in the fish with mixture after patting the fish dry with kitchen paper towels.
3. Heat frying pan. Add enough oil for frying.
4. Fry fish in very hot oil. Turn fish over to fry the other side when one side is done. Serve.

SAMBAL IKAN
(Fish Sambal)

4 chubb mackeral (kembung)
8 shallots
4 pips garlic
5 dried red chillies
4 fresh red chillies
½ tsp shrimp paste (belacan)
1 tbsp sugar
1 tbsp tamarind paste (assam jawa)
1 stalk lemon grass (serai)
11 tbsp cooking oil
Salt to taste

PREPARATION

1. Remove gills and intestines of fish. Clean and drain.
2. Slice shallots and garlic.
3. Soak dried chillies in warm water for 15 minutes. Pound fresh and dried chillies finely.
4. Add shallots and garlic to chillies, pound finely.
5. Dissolve tamarind paste in 1 cup water. Remove seeds. Drain.
6. Bruise lemon grass.

METHOD

1. Add oil to heated frying pan.
2. Fry fish until fairly brown. Set aside. Discard oil.
3. Using fresh oil, fry pounded ingredients, lemon grass, shrimp paste until fragrant.
4. Add tamarind juice, sugar and salt to taste.
5. When gravy is boiling, add fish.
6. Cook on medium heat until gravy starts to thicken. Serve.

SAMBAL IKAN: A trio of chubb mackeral fried, smothered with a hot sambal and served in boat-shaped dishes — an unique presentation to augment your nasi lemak buffet.

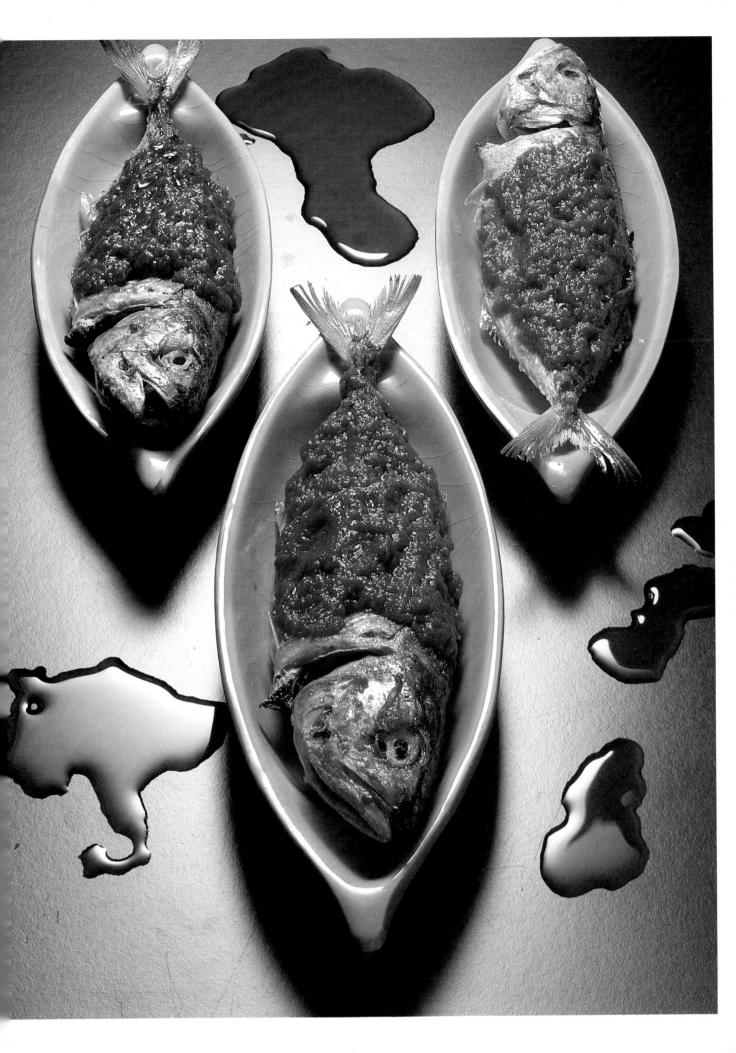

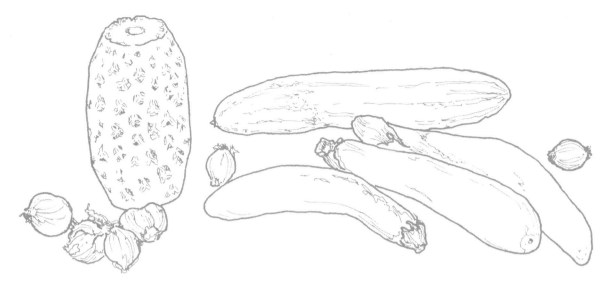

SAMBAL BELACAN BRINJALS

300 g brinjals (long purple ones)
2 shallots
3 pips garlic
2 tbsp oil

PREPARATION

1. Slice off both ends of brinjals.
2. Mince garlic and slice shallots finely.

METHOD

1. Heat oil in frying pan and put in whole brinjals. Simmer with frying pan lid on, lifting to turn brinjals every now and then.
2. When brown and cooked (takes from 7 – 10 minutes) remove from pan. Peel off skin and cut into 5 centimetre slices at a slant.
3. In the remaining oil, fry onions and garlic until fragrant. Set aside.
4. To serve, garnish brinjal slices with shallots and garlic. Eat with sambal belacan. (see page 61).

Note:

Brinjals will turn soft if you fry it long enough in oil.

Variations:

Do not slice brinjals when they are cooked. Instead, remove skin and using a fork, spread out the brinjals and mix a sambal belacan with a dash of light soya sauce and lime juice into the brinjals. Serve.

Alternately, fry some minced garlic in 3 – 4 tablespoonfuls of lard. Add some light soya sauce, pepper, seasoning and sliced red chillies. Combine above with brinjals and omit the sambal belacan.

SAMBAL TIMUN AND NANAS
(Cucumber and Pineapple Sambal)

1 small pineapple
1 cucumber
4 fresh red chillies
2 tbsp shrimp paste (belacan)
1 tbsp thick dark soya sauce
2 tbsp sugar

PREPARATION

1. Skin and clean pineapple. Quarter lengthwise and cut into triangular pieces.
2. Skin cucumber. Cut into four pieces lengthwise, remove core. Cut diagonally into pieces 1 cm thick.
3. Pound chillies finely.

METHOD

1. Toast shrimp paste after pressing into wafer-thin piece. Alternately, heat in frying pan till crumbly and fragrant. Add belacan to pounded chillies and pound again till well mixed.
2. Scoop sufficient quantity of cucumber and pineapple into bowl.
3. Top with required amount of pounded ingredients, soya sauce and sugar.

Note:

If you wish to you could add the soya sauce and sugar into pounded ingredients and stir to blend well.

CHINCHALOK WITH CHILLIES

Chinchalok, pickled shrimps, is a delicacy eaten with chillies, shallots and lime juice. Since it is very fishy, it is an acquired taste.

Chinchalok (available bottled locally)
7 shallots
2 fresh red chillies
1 or 2 big limes

PREPARATION

1. Slice chillies and shallots finely.
2. Squeeze juice of one lime.

METHOD

1. Scoop about 5 tablespoonfuls of chinchalok onto a small plate.
2. Squeeze lime juice into shallots and chillies and mix well.
3. Add the required amount of mixture to chinchalok and serve.

Note:
If mixture is not sour enough, add juice from remaining lime. Use as a dip or with rice.

SAMBAL BELACAN

5 fresh red chillies
1 tbsp shrimp paste (belacan)
1 big lime
Salt to taste

METHOD

1. Press shrimp paste between thumb and forefinger into thin wafer and toast over low fire till brown. Alternatively, heat in a frying pan and press with a ladle until it crumbles.
2. Pound chillies finely. Add shrimp paste and pound again till well mixed.
3. Remove, add salt to taste, squeeze in lime juice and mix well. Serve.

Note:
Pressing the shrimp paste into a thin wafer will ensure that it is well cooked. A thick piece will take longer to heat up and will lack fragrance. If heating in a frying pan, put on a low flame and crumble it. It may stick to the sides of the pan but you can scrape it up with a spoon.

SAMBAL BENDI
(Lady's Fingers Sambal)

300 g lady's fingers (bendi), choose young ones
50 – 70 g dried prawns
4 shallots
2 big limes
4 fresh chillies
2 tsp shrimp paste (belacan)

PREPARATION

1. Cut away both ends of lady's fingers, wash, drain.
2. Remove shells and heads of prawns. Wash, drain and pound coarsely.
3. Slice shallots finely.
4. Cut limes into quarters. Squeeze one lime for juice.
5. Pound chillies finely.

METHOD

1. Press shrimp paste into a thin wafer and toast well. Alternately crumble it in a frying pan. Add toasted shrimp paste to pounded chillies and pound again till chillies and shrimp paste are well mixed.
2. Bring 3 – 4 rice bowls of water to boil. Add pinch or two of salt and scald lady's fingers in it. When soft, drain and set aside.
3. Mix pounded chillies, dried prawns and shallots.
4. Add in juice of cut lime and mix well.
5. Serve with lady's fingers. If sambal is not sour enough, add juice from remaining lime.

SAMBAL BENDI: Served whole or sliced, this dish of lady's fingers and dried prawn sambal is a delicious side dish. Though simple, its flavour is full bodied. Give it an added lift with the liberal use of lime juice.

SAMBAL UDANG PETAI: Cooked with an extremely full-flavoured bean, this dish may not be everyone's cup of tea. Petai is believed to be of medicinal value and helpful to diabetics.

SAMBAL UDANG PETAI
(Prawn Sambal with Petai)

300 g medium-sized prawns
A few strings petai
1 stalk lemon grass (serai)
5 dried chillies
Thumb-sized piece fresh young turmeric (kunyit)
5 shallots
3 pips garlic
1 tbsp tamarind paste assam jawa
1 tsp shrimp paste (belacan)
A few stalks mint leaves (daun pudina)
10 tbsp cooking oil
Salt

PREPARATION

1. Shell, clean and drain prawns.
2. Cut lemon grass into slices.
3. Soak dried chillies in warm water for 15 minutes.
4. Pound lemon grass and chillies finely.
5. Skin turmeric. Add to pounded lemon grass and chillies and pound all three finely.
6. Cut shallots into small slices and slice garlic finely. Add to above pounded ingredients and pound again.
7. Dissolve tamarind paste in 1 – 1½ rice bowls of water. Remove seeds and strain. Set aside.
8. Discard main stalk of mint leaves, wash and drain the rest.
9. Discard petai stalks and take out beans, clean.

METHOD

1. Add oil to heated frying pan. Add pounded ingredients and shrimp paste.
2. Stir till fragrant; control heat. Add prawns and petai beans. Stir for 1 – 2 minutes.
3. Add tamarind juice, cook until gravy is quite thick.
4. Add salt to taste. Slow boil till prawns are cooked.
5. Add mint leaves.
6. Simmer for 10 – 15 minutes. Serve.

Note:
Petai is a pungent bean with a strong flavour. It is definately an acquired taste.

Poultry

As with fish, the nyonyas have elaborate ways of preparing poultry. Aside from using chicken in their gulais, it is also deep fried and roasted. This is often done after marinating it in generous amounts of rempah and shredded aromatic leaves. Examples of these are Ayam Limau Purut, Hot Spiced Chicken and Sar Keong Chicken. You can be certain that poultry dishes prepared nyonya style are never boring nor dull.

HOT SPICE CHICKEN

1½ kg chicken

2 tbsp coriander (ketumbar)	
1 tsp cummin seeds (jintan putih)	
10 white peppercorns	(A) Ground finely
Thumbsized piece fresh young turmeric (kunyit)	
Thumbsized piece ginger	

6 fresh red chillies	
5 shallots	(B) Ground
3 pips garlic	or pounded finely
1 small stalk lemon grass (serai)	

1 coconut, grated
10 tbsp cooking oil
Salt to taste

PREPARATION

1. Cut chicken into fairly big pieces.
2. Add 2½ to 3 rice bowls of water to grated coconut to squeeze for milk.
3. Grind (A) and (B) separately.

METHOD

1. Heat oil in frying pan. Add pounded ground ingredients. Stir for 2 minutes.
2. Reduce heat to minimum, add part of the coconut milk and stir until fragrant and the ingredients bubble in the oil.
3. Add chicken pieces and 2 tablespoonfuls salt. Stir well so that chicken is coated with fried ingredients.
4. Add remaining coconut milk and boil till chicken is cooked. Bring up heat and stir until the mixture is dry. Dish out. Serve.

SAR KEONG CHICKEN/DUCK

1 young duck or chicken about 1½ kg in weight, cleaned and cut into fairly large pieces.
3 tbsp preserved soya bean paste (taucheong)

10 shallots, sliced	
5 pips garlic	Pounded finely
7 cm piece fresh galangal (lengkuas)	

12 tbsp cooking oil
1 tsp thick dark soya sauce
1 tbsp light soya sauce
1 tsp pepper
Monosodium glutamate (optional)

METHOD

1. Heat a frying pan, add oil. When oil is hot, add pounded ingredients, preserved soya bean paste, pepper and monosodium glutamate (optional). Stir until fragrant.
2. Add duck or chicken pieces, light soya sauce and thick dark soya sauce.
3. Stir for 2 to 3 minutes. Add water till duck or chicken pieces are covered. Boil and stir often.
4. If cooking duck, check for water level since gravy could well dry up as duck takes longer to cook.
5. When meat is about to cook, allow gravy to evaporate till dish is dry. Remove from heat. Serve.

AYAM PANGGANG SATAY
(Roast Chicken)

1.5 kg chicken

4 tbsp coriander (ketumbar)	
1 tbsp fennel seeds (jintan manis)	
½ tsp cummin seeds (jintan putih)	
3.5 cm ginger	
1½ cm fresh young turmeric (kunyit)	Ground
7 shallots	finely
3 pips garlic	
1 stalk lemon grass (serai)	
6 dried chillies	

½ coconut, grated
1 tsp salt
Monosodium glutamate/Seasoning (optional)

PREPARATION

1. Clean chicken and leave to hang in a dry airy place.
2. Soak dried chillies in warm water for 15 minutes.
3. Add ½ rice bowl of water to grated coconut and squeeze for first milk.

METHOD

1. Add coconut milk and salt to ground ingredients. Mix well.
2. Rub mixture thoroughly on chicken, both inside and out. Season for ½ to ¾ of an hour.
3. Heat oven to 121°C (250°F). Roast chicken for 1½ to 2 hours till golden brown. Serve hot.

AYAM KUNING (KUNYIT)
(Turmeric Chicken)

4 big chicken pieces
1 stalk lemon grass (serai)
20 white peppercorns
2 pieces thumbsized dried turmeric (kunyit)
3 fresh red chillies
½ tsp salt
1 rice bowl cooking oil

PREPARATION

1. Pound lemon grass, peppercorns, chillies and kunyit finely.
2. Clean chicken, wash, drain and marinate with the pounded ingredients and salt for 1 hour.

METHOD

1. Heat pan, add 1 rice bowl of cooking oil. When oil is hot, put in the chicken pieces. Stir well.
2. Reduce heat to low. Cover pan. Stir once in a while until chicken pieces are cooked.
3. Dish out and serve.

FRIED CHICKEN NYONYA STYLE

1 chicken about 1¼ kg in weight. Discard neck and head, clean and cut into 6 big pieces. Drain.

1½ tsp pepper
1½ tsp dark soya sauce
1 tsp light soya sauce
1 tbsp sugar   Mixed together into a bowl
1 tsp sesame oil
½ tsp salt

1½ – 2 rice bowls cooking oil

METHOD

1. Season chicken pieces with mixed ingredients, taking care to marinade well. Leave for 1 hour.
2. Heat a frying pan. Add oil. Fry chicken pieces in oil for two minutes, then stir well.
3. Reduce heat to medium. Cover but stir often till cooked. Serve.

CHICKEN INNARDS FRIED WITH CUCUMBER

200 g chicken innards (including livers, kidneys, intestines)
1 cucumber
1 big red onion
1 fresh chilli
2 pips garlic
2 tsp sugar
1 tsp light soya sauce
1 tbsp vinegar
¼ tsp pepper
1½ tsp cornflour
Salt to taste
5 tbsp cooking oil

PREPARATION

1. Slit open chicken intestines with a sharp knife, put in a bowl, add 2 teaspoonfuls salt and 1 tablespoonful vinegar. Rub well with your fingers to get rid of the smell. Wash in water and cut into 5 centimetre lengths.
2. Clean livers and cut into slices 1.5 centimetres thick.
3. Clean kidneys and cut into slices.
4. Skin cucumber, cut into quarters, lengthwise. Remove core then slice at a slant.
5. Peel onion skin and cut into quarters.
6. Cut chilli into half then slice at a slant.
7. Mince garlic coarsely.

METHOD

1. Heat pan, add oil. When oil is hot, add garlic and onion, stir for 1 minute. Add intestines and kidneys, stir until ¼ cooked. Add ⅓ rice bowl water, fry until ¾ cooked.
2. Add cucumber, liver, light soya sauce, sugar, pepper, vinegar and salt to taste.
3. Meanwhile put 1½ teaspoonfuls cornflour into a small bowl, add 2 – 3 tablespoonfuls water to dissolve it.
4. When the dish is cooked pour in the cornflour, stir till it starts to thicken. Dish out and garnish with spring onion cut into 5 centimetre lengths. Serve.

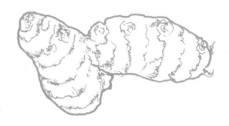

AYAM LIMAU PURUT
(Limau Purut Chicken)

1 kg chicken

10 shallots
1 stalk lemon grass (serai)
3 pips garlic
6 dried chillies
5 fresh red chillies
3.5 cm fresh young turmeric (kunyit)

Pounded
till fairly fine

Thumbsized galangal (lengkuas)
3 daun limau purut
1½ tamarind pieces (assam keping)
9 tbsp cooking oil
½ a big coconut, grated

AYAM LIMAU PURUT: The unmistakable tastes and fragrances of tamarind, daun limau purut and lemon grass combine to give this curry a special taste.

PREPARATION

1. Clean chicken and cut into pieces.
2. Smash galangal with flat side of cleaver.
3. Soak dried chillies in warm water for 15 minutes.
4. Add 1 rice bowl of water to grated coconut to squeeze for first milk. Add again 1½ rice bowls of water to squeeze for second milk.

METHOD

1. Heat kuali or pot till hot. Add cooking oil. Add pounded ingredients. Stir until fragrant.
2. Add chicken and half of the second milk. Stir for five minutes.
3. Add remaining second coconut milk and all of the first coconut milk, tamarind, galangal and daun limau purut. Stir and add salt to taste. Cover pot or kuali to cook dish.
4. Turn to medium heat, stirring once in a while; simmer till cooked.

ENCHE KEBIN

ENCHE KEBIN: This version of the famous chicken dish has a light gravy for a change.

½ chicken
2 potatoes
1 small carrot
75 g snow peas
1 big red onion
1 tbsp light soya sauce
1 piece fresh ginger
1 rice bowl of water
¼ tsp salt
½ tsp cornflour
7 tbsp cooking oil
Monosodium glutamate/Seasoning (optional)

PREPARATION

1. Clean chicken, rub over with 1 teaspoonful salt. Season for 40 minutes.
2. Skin and clean potatoes, cut into slices. Soak in water in which a little salt had been dissolved.
3. Skin onion and cut into rings.
4. Skin carrot, clean and cut into small decorative shapes.
5. Skin, wash and pound ginger finely; squeeze out 1 teaspoonful of juice.
6. Mix the cornflour with 1 tablespoonful water till smooth.

METHOD

1. Deep fry chicken in hot oil on medium heat till brown. Remove, cool and cut into pieces.
2. In the same oil deep fry potatoes till brown. Remove and set aside.
3. Dish out the oil leaving about 7 tablespoonfuls. Add onion, fry until soft.
4. Add 1 rice bowl of water, light soya sauce, 1 teaspoonful ginger juice, cut carrot, ¼ teaspoonful salt and a little seasoning and monosodium glutamate.
5. Slow boil until carrot is soft.
6. Add fried chicken, snow peas and fried potatoes. Stir well, add cornflour solution, stir again for a few minutes and dish out. Serve.

Pork

Pork is regularly featured in the nyonya diet,
whether it be stewed, fried or curried. There are
interesting and ingenious ways of using pork:
simmered in some sauce, stir fried with salted
cabbage or preserved soya bean or perhaps minced
and steamed. Whatever the method, nyonya pork
dishes are especially appetising and inviting.

PORK SATAY

600 g pork
40 'lidi' sticks (ribs of coconut fronds)

SEASONING INGREDIENTS
6 shallots
4 pips garlic
1 tsp ground coriander (ketumbar)   Ground
¼ tsp ground cummin seeds (jintan putih)   finely
Thumb-sized fresh turmeric (kunyit)

½ tsp salt
1 big lime
4 tbsp coconut milk
1 tsp sugar

PREPARATION

1. Wash the pork and drain well. Cut into small pieces for sticking into skewers of coconut frond ribs.
2. Marinate pork pieces in the ground ingredients, sugar, salt, coconut milk and juice of 1 big lime. Mix well and season for 2 hours.
3. Pierce cut meat onto the sharpened skewers.

SAUCE

150 g groundnuts
8 dried chillies soaked in warm water for 15 minutes
5 shallots
4 pips garlic
1 stalk lemon grass (serai)
Thumbsized fresh turmeric (kunyit)
3 tbsp coriander (ketumbar)
1½ tsp cummin seeds (jintan putih)
½ coconut, grated
1 tsp shrimp paste (belacan)
Sugar and salt to taste

PREPARATION

1. Fry groundnuts on low heat without oil until brown, stirring continuously. Cool, skin and pound coarsely.
2. Grind coriander and cummin seeds finely.
3. Grind shallots, garlic, lemon grass and turmeric finely. Add shrimp paste and mix well.
4. Grind chillies finely.
5. Add 2 rice bowls of water to grated coconut to squeeze for milk.

METHOD

1. Heat pan, add 10 tablespoonfuls cooking oil. When oil is hot, add all ground ingredients and fry until fragrant, add a little coconut milk while stirring so that the mixture will not burn or dry up.
2. Add remaining coconut milk, sugar and salt to taste and bring to boil. The sauce should be slightly on the sweet side.
3. Add pounded groundnuts, stir to mix well. Dish out.
4. Barbeque meat over grill or charcoal fire. See that the charcoal is red hot before grilling. If not, the satay will have a smoky taste. Turn over often to prevent burning.
5. Remove when meat is cooked.
6. Serve with sauce, cut cucumber slices and raw onions.

Note:

Finely chopped pineapple may be added in the sauce. Select streaky pork for this satay. Skewer strips of fat between lean meat.

Rice cake or ketupat can be made by packing rice in cloth bags and boiling till cooked. Remove from bags and cube.

PORK SATAY: Nyonya pork satay is a Baba's favourite. Always grill over glowing ambers of a charcoal fire for the taste to come through.

BAH YWE PHO IN TAUCHEONG
(Fried Lard Crusts in Soya Bean Paste)

300 g pork fat
2 green chillies
3 fresh red chillies
6 sour starfruit (belimbing)
150 g prawns
1 tbsp preserved soya bean paste (taucheong)
4 shallots
2 pips garlic
Sugar to taste
Dark soya sauce
6 tbsp cooking oil

PREPARATION

1. Cut pork fat into 2 centimetre cubes. Fry at a low heat until it gives out oil. Stir often until cubes shrink and turn brown. Remove heat and dish out the lard crusts. Set aside.
2. Pound shallots and garlic finely.
3. Pound red chillies finely.
4. Shell prawns; wash and drain.
5. Quarter green and red chillies lengthwise.
6. Cut sour starfruits into bitesize pieces.

METHOD

1. Dish out the pork oil, leaving 6 tablespoonfuls and the lard crusts. Heat the oil again until hot.
2. Add pounded shallots, preserved soya bean paste and pounded chilli and stir for half a minute; then add prawns and sour starfruit, stir another 1 minute.
3. Add ½ a rice bowl of water, a few drops dark soya sauce and sugar to taste, bring to slow boil until sour starfruits are soft. If gravy is too thick, add a bit more water but the dish should not be too watery.
4. Add cut red and green chillies and stir for ½ a minute more. Remove from heat. Dish out and serve.

PORK LEG IN BLACK VINEGAR

1 fore-leg of pork, chopped
300 g young ginger
1 rice bowl of Chinese black vinegar
3 tbsp sugar
1 tbsp dark soya sauce
1 tbsp light soya sauce
3 eggs
3 pips garlic, minced
Cooking oil

PREPARATION

1. Clean pork pieces. Wash and drain.
2. Remove skin of ginger and pound to break open.
3. Hard boil eggs. Shell.
4. Put ginger in pot, add water to cover ginger. Boil for 5 minutes. Discard the water and set aside the ginger.

METHOD

1. Heat pot, add 4 tablespoonfuls cooking oil. When oil is hot, add minced garlic, stir until soft; add pork pieces and stir for 5 minutes.
2. Add 3½ rice bowls of water, black vinegar, sugar, dark soya sauce, hard boiled eggs and ½ teaspoonful salt.
3. Simmer until the pork is soft.
4. Remove from heat and serve.

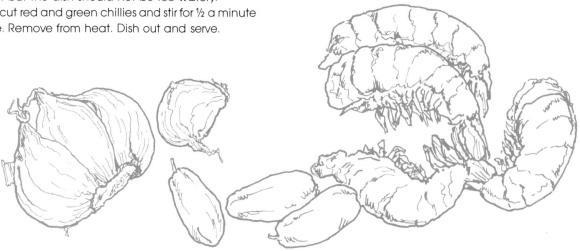

FRIED KIAM CHAI WITH PORK
(Fried Salted Cabbage with Pork)

300 g salted cabbage (kiam chai)
125 g streaky pork
Thumb-sized piece ginger
3 pips garlic
2 shallots
1 tbsp sugar
8 tbsp cooking oil
1 tbsp light soya sauce
Thick dark soya sauce

PREPARATION

1. Cut salted cabbage into small pieces. Soak in water for a little while to remove excessive saltiness.
2. Cut the pork into fine slices.
3. Shred ginger.
4. Mince garlic.
5. Slice onions finely.

METHOD

1. Heat oil in frying pan. Add garlic and shallots. Stir for a minute.
2. Add ginger and pork. Stir for two more minutes and add salted cabbage.
3. Add a few drops of dark soya sauce, light soya sauce and sugar. Add a tablespoonful or so of water for a little gravy.
4. Stir until salted cabbage is soft and fragrant. Turn heat to low so that gravy will not evaporate.
5. Serve.

PORK STEAMED WITH SALTED EGG

1 salted egg
1 chicken egg
225 g pork
Pinch of pepper
5 tbsp water

PREPARATION

1. Clean pork and mince.
2. Break the salted egg into a bowl, stir. Then break in the chicken egg.
3. Put in the minced pork, mix well with the eggs.
4. Add 5 tablespoonfuls water to mixture and beat well.

METHOD

1. Pour the pork and egg mixture into a deep steaming bowl. Cover with a plate to prevent water vapour from entering while steaming.
2. Add water to a pan, place the bowl of pork and egg mixture in the pot making sure water level is below bowl.
3. Cover pot and steam dish for 20 minutes.
4. Remove heat when cooked. Serve.

Note:
Test by pushing fork or chopstick into the mixture to see whether the dish is cooked.

PORK PATTIES

600 g lean pork

1 tsp five spice powder (ng heong fun)
1 level tsp pepper
3 tbsp flour
1 tsp sesame oil   (A)
1 tbsp light soya sauce
½ tsp salt
2 tbsp water

2 big red onions
75 g snow peas
1 tomato
Monosodium glutamate/seasoning (optional)
Oil for deep frying

PREPARATION

1. Wash, drain pork and mince finely.
2. Cut onions into rings.
3. Cut tomato into slices.
4. Add (A) to the minced pork. Mix well.

METHOD

1. Make patties of pork mixture.
2. In about 10 tablespoonfuls hot oil, deep fry the patties. Drain. Set aside.
3. Dish out the oil leaving about 2 tablespoonfuls, add onions and snow peas, fry till cooked. Dish out and garnish patties together with tomato slices.

SWEET AND SOUR SPARE RIBS: Spare ribs, a favoured cut of pork in nyonya cooking is given the familiar Chinese treatment.

SWEET SOUR SPARE RIBS

300 g fleshly spare ribs
1½ tbsp sour plum sauce (suin muei cheo)
¾ tbsp preserved soya bean paste (taucheong)   *1 tbsp*
¾ tbsp sugar
1 tsp light soya sauce
5 shallots   *2*
3 pips garlic   *6-7 - Pound*
2 slices ginger
1 fresh red chilli   *2-3*
8 tbsp cooking oil
assam water.   *water.*

PREPARATION

1. Wash and chop spare ribs. Drain.
2. Mince chilli.
3. Pound shallots, garlic and ginger finely.
4. Dissolve 1 teaspoonful cornflour in 1½ tablespoonfuls water.

METHOD

1. Heat pan, add oil. When oil is hot add pounded onions, garlic and ginger; stir until fragrant.
2. Add preserved soya bean paste and spare ribs, stir for ½ a minute.
3. Add 1½ rice bowls of water, sour plum sauce, light soya sauce, chilli and sugar.
4. Simmer until spare ribs are cooked. Add cornflour.
5. When gravy starts to thicken, remove from heat. Dish out and serve.

TAU YEW BAK
(Pork in soya sauce)

300 g streaky pork
2 pieces soya bean cakes (taukua)
3 eggs, hardboiled
3 pips garlic
1½ tbsp thick dark soya sauce
1 rice bowl of water
4 tbsp cooking oil
Salt and sugar to taste
Pepper
Monosodium glutamate/seasoning (optional)

PREPARATION

1. Cut pork into big cubes.
2. Cut Soya bean cakes into quarters diagonally.
3. Remove shell of eggs.
4. Crush garlic with side of a cleaver. Leave garlic skin intact (optional).

METHOD

1. Heat cooking oil in pot. Add garlic. Stir for a minute, then add pork and a little pepper.
2. Stir for two to three minutes. Add water and dark soya sauce. Stir slowly until sauce dissolves.
3. Add eggs, soya bean cakes, sugar and salt to taste. Boil for a few minutes, then simmer on low heat. Serve.

HONG BAK
(Braised pork)

300 g pork, cut into large cubes

9 shallots
4 pips garlic
2.5 cm piece ginger   Pounded
2 heaped tbsp coriander (ketumbar)   finely
3 pieces dry or 4 pieces fresh cekur
30 white pepper corns

3 eggs, hard boiled, shelled
1½ tbsp preserved soya bean paste (taucheong)
1½ to 2 rice bowls of water
9 tbsp cooking oil
Salt to taste
Pepper (optional)
Monosodium glutamate/seasoning (optional)

METHOD

1. Heat pot. Add cooking oil. When oil is hot reduce heat to medium. Add pounded ingredients and preserved soya bean paste.
2. Stir until fragrant. Add pork cubes. Stir for a while, then add water. Add salt to taste.
3. Add hard boiled eggs and allow dish to simmer until pork is cooked. Serve with rice.

Seafood

"They never leave their fish alone" is one oft made comment of the nyonya cook. Since steaming and boiling were considered too boring and unexciting, fish in a nyonya dish was usually "dressed" up. Favourite ways being to rempah, sambal and assam seafood. Other tantilising methods involve marinating in fragrant pounded mixtures, smothering in thick rich gravies or stuffing with ground root and herb mixtures. Not surprising then, after such caring efforts, fish dishes in the nyonya kitchen were always at their flavoursome best.

Prawns were also given similar elaborate treatment and nothing can surpass the simple yet gratifying delightful meal of prawn fritters, sambal belacan and fried soya bean cake.

SWEET SOUR CRAB

600 g land crab
Thumb-sized ginger, shredded
3 shallots
4 pips garlic
1 big fresh red chilli
1 tbsp light soya sauce
½ tbsp sugar
1 tbsp vinegar
1 stalk Chinese celery (daun salderi/kun choy)
5 tbsp oil
1 tsp cornflour

PREPARATION

1. Remove shell of crab. Clean and cut into quarters.
2. Slice shallots and mince the garlic.
3. Slice chilli at a slant.
4. Dissolve 1 heaped teaspoonful cornflour in 5 tablespoonfuls water. Add 1 tablespoonful vinegar and 1 tablespoonful sugar. Stir well.
5. Cut Chinese celery into 5 centimetre lengths.

METHOD

1. Heat pan, add 5 tablespoonfuls oil. When oil is hot, add garlic, ginger and shallots. Stir till soft.
2. Add crab, stir a while and cover, keep stirring often until crabs turn reddish and is cooked. Remove cover.
3. Add ½ rice bowl water, 1 tablespoonful light soya sauce, 2 tablespoonfuls tomato sauce, sliced chilli and Chinese celery. Stir a while then add the cornflour solution. Quickly stir until gravy starts to thicken.
4. Remove heat and dish out. Serve.

SWEET SOUR FISH

450 g Chinese pomfret (bawal puteh)

SAUCE INGREDIENTS
4 tbsp tomato sauce
2 tsp light soya sauce
1 tsp sugar
1 flat tsp preserved soya bean paste (taucheong)
1 fresh red chilli
½ big onion
½ tsp corn flour
1½ tbsp water
1 rice bowl water
5 tbsp cooking oil

GARNISHING
Some coriander leaves (daun ketumbar/yin sai)

PREPARATION

1. Clean fish, wash and drain.
2. Pound chilli finely.
3. Cut onion into small pieces.
4. Mix corn flour with water until a smooth consistency is obtained.

METHOD

1. Steam fish in a plate for 5 to 10 minutes until cooked. Remove and set aside.
2. Heat kuali, add 5 tablespoonfuls cooking oil. When oil is hot, add cut onion, fry for a minute or two till soft.
3. Add preserved soya bean paste, fry for another minute.
4. Add 1 cup water, 4 tablespoonfuls tomato sauce, 2 teaspoonfuls light soya sauce and sugar to taste. Slow boil for a few minutes.
5. Add corn flour mixture, stir quickly for a few minutes.
6. Remove gravy and pour over the steamed fish.
7. Garnish with coriander leaves and serve.

Note:
You can substitute cuttlefish for fish in this dish. Use 300 g parboiled cuttlefish.

SWEET SOUR CRAB: A dish which enjoys star status.

IKAN PARI FRIED IN KIAM CHAI
(Stingray fried in Salted Cabbage)

300 g stingray (ikan pari)
300 g salted cabbage (kiam chai)
2 fresh red chillies
3 shallots
3 pips garlic
Thumb-sized piece ginger
1 tbsp sugar (optional)
1 tbsp pepper
½ tbsp thick dark soya sauce
7 tbsp cooking oil

PREPARATION

1. Slice chillies finely and discard seeds.
2. Slice shallots finely and mince garlic.
3. Cut stingray into small pieces. Wash and drain.
4. Cut salted cabbage into small pieces or shreds. Soak in water for 10 – 15 minutes if it is the very salty variety. Drain.

METHOD

1. Heat frying pan. Add oil. When oil is hot, add ginger, shallots and garlic. Stir till light brown.
2. Add stingray. Stir for 3 minutes. Add salted cabbage, stir till fragrant.
3. Add water for gravy and also thick dark soya sauce. Add pepper then sugar.
4. Stir, then cover till salted cabbage is soft. Test gravy for sweetness and saltiness. Adjust taste.
5. When ready, the salted cabbage should just be wet and not too much gravy should remain. If it is too dry, the fish will not taste good.
6. Adjust by adding water if required. Serve hot.

CHILLI FISH

2 horse mackeral (selar)
5 small shallots
4 pips garlic
5 fresh red chillies
1 tsp shrimp paste (belacan)
1 tbsp tamarind paste (assam jawa)
1 tbsp sugar
Pinch of salt
Monosodium glutamate/seasoning (optional)
8 tbsp oil
A sprig of spring onion, cut into 5 cm lengths

PREPARATION

1. Discard unwanted parts of fish, wash and drain.
2. Pound shallots and garlic finely.
3. Pound chillies and shrimp paste finely.
4. Dissolve tamarind paste in 1 rice bowl water and strain for juice.

METHOD

1. Heat pan, add oil. When oil is hot, add the two pounded ingredients.
2. Fry until fragrant. Add tamarind juice, sugar, pinch of salt and seasoning to taste. Add fish.
3. Simmer until fish is cooked.
4. Dish out and garnish with spring onions. Serve.

ASSAM FISH
(Tamarind Fish)

300 g hard tail or chubb mackerel (cencaru or kembung)
2 stalks lemon grass (serai)
2 fresh red chillies
1 tbsp tamarind paste (assam jawa)
½ tsp shrimp paste (belacan)
½ big red onion
Monosodium glutamate/seasoning (optional)
Salt to taste

PREPARATION

1. Clean fish. Wash and drain.
2. Slit open chillies. Remove seeds.
3. Bruise lemon grass.
4. Dissolve shrimp paste in 2¼ rice bowls of water. Strain for juice.
5. Cut ½ onion into two.

METHOD

1. Pour tamarind juice in a pot and heat. Add lemon grass, ½ teaspoonful shrimp paste, chillies and onions.
2. Bring to boil when gravy is fragrant, add seasoning and salt to taste.
3. Add fish; when cooked remove from heat and serve.

Note:

A tamarind piece can also be used instead of tamarind paste. Remember to taste gravy when it is boiling. When gravy is sour enough remove the tamarind piece. If left too long the gravy will be very sour.

KIAM HU CHAR
(Fried Salt Fish)

150 –200 g salt fish flesh (without bones) or 2 small whole
  salt fish
3 – 4 tbsp cooking oil

PREPARATION

1. Cut fish flesh into pieces of 1.5 cm thickness. For whole
    salt fish, scrape off scales and remove intestines. Soak
    salt fish flesh in cold water for 10 – 15 minutes.
2. Clean after draining and pat dry with kitchen paper
    towels.

METHOD

1. Heat a frying pan. Add cooking oil. Fry salt fish.
2. Then reduce heat to medium to prevent fish from
    getting burnt.
3. Keep turning often till it turns fairly brown and crisp.
    Remove and serve.

Note:
Make sure salt fish flesh is patted dry before frying or it will
not turn out crisp; moreover the oil will splutter if any water
is retained in the fish.

For added fragrance to this simple yet delectable
appetizer, fry together:
2 – 3 pips sliced garlic;
3 small sliced onions;
3 – 4 fresh red chillies, sliced or dried chillies, soaked in
warm water for 15 minutes; and a 2.5 cm piece of ginger,
finely shredded.

Put salt fish in a steaming tray or porcelain bowl. Pour
fried ingredients together with a generous portion of oil
over salt fish and steam.

IKAN MASAK ASSAM KICAP
(Fish in Assam sauce)

8 Hardtail (cencaru)
2 big stalks lemon grass (serai), bruised
1 piece tamarind (assam keping)
1½ tbsp dark soya sauce
1 rice bowl of water
2 tbsp light soya sauce
Sugar and salt to taste
A pinch of Monosodium glutamate (optional)

PREPARATION

1. Remove scales, gills and intestines of fish. Leave
    heads intact. Season with 1½ teaspoon salt for 15
    minutes.

METHOD

1. Heat a pot. Add water, soya sauces, lemon grass and
    tamarind piece; bring to boil.
2. Add fish and chillies. Boil till fish is cooked.
3. Add sugar, salt and seasoning (optional) to taste.
    Serve.

Note:
Cook on medium flame or dish will burn.

IKAN PANGGANG
(Grilled Fish)

600 g stingray (ikan pari)
10 shallots
3 fresh red chillies
1 tbsp shrimp paste (belacan)
2 big limes
1 tbsp dark soya sauce
1 tsp light soya sauce
2 tbsp sugar
¼ rice bowl boiled water
Banana leaves

PREPARATION

1. Cut stingray into 3 slices lengthwise. Clean, wash and
    drain.
2. Soak banana leaves in boiling water till soft. Remove
    and clean.
3. Wrap each piece of stingray in 2 to 3 layers of banana
    leaves.

METHOD

1. Place wrapped stingray in a pan with 3 tbsp oil.
2. Cover and fry over low flame.
3. Keep turning often until fish is cooked. It may take
    about 20 minutes. Remove and serve with sauce.

SAUCE:
1. Slice shallots finely.
2. Slice chillies.
3. Fry shrimp paste over low heat until dry and powdery,
    dish out.
4. Put cut shallots, chillies, fried shrimp paste, dark soya
    sauce, light soya sauce, sugar and lime juice into a
    bowl. Add ¼ rice bowls of boiled water and stir well till
    sugar dissolves. Serve with fish.

(OVERLEAF) *IKAN PANGGANG*

IKAN ASSAM PEDAS
(Hot and Sour Fish)

4 chubb mackeral (kembung)

6 shallots
2.5 cm fresh turmeric (kunyit), skinned
1 stalk lemon grass (serai), sliced finely   (A)
5 red chillies, deseeded

Thumb-sized piece shrimp paste (belacan)
1½ pieces tamarind (assam gelugor)
4 stalks polygonum (daun kesum)
1 phaeomaria (bunga kantan)
3 rice bowls water
Salt and sugar to taste
Monosodium glutamate (optional)

PREPARATION

1. Clean fish and discard gills and intestines.
2. Wash polygonum, discard stalks.
3. Cut phaeomaria into quarters.
4. Pound (A) finely.

METHOD

1. Pour water into pot. Add pounded ingredients, tamarind pieces, shrimp paste, polygonum and phaeomaria.
2. Use a spoon to dissolve shrimp paste.
3. Bring to boil for a few minutes until the soup is fragrant.
4. Add a little sugar and salt to taste. Then add fish. After it boils, simmer on low heat. Serve.

PEE HU CHAR
(Preserved Fish with Vegetables)

150 g preserved fish (pee hu)
150 g pork
1 small yambean (sengkuang)
3 – 4 dry mushrooms
75 g snow peas
1 small carrot
75 g cauliflower
120 g white cabbage
1 big red onion
3 pips garlic, minced
8 tbsp cooking oil
Salt to taste

PREPARATION

1. Cut carrot into small, decorative shapes, cauliflower into small pieces and cabbage into cubes.
2. Soak preserved fish for 15 minutes in ½ a rice bowl of water, discard bones and cut into small pieces. Do not discard water.
3. Cut pork into big cubes.
4. Soak mushrooms until soft, cut into small pieces.
5. Slice off top of onion. Cut into quarters.
6. Cut yambean into thin squares.

METHOD

1. Heat frying pan. Add oil. When hot, fry onions and garlic. Stir fry for one minute before adding pork. Stir for another minute.
2. Add preserved fish, yambean and carrot. Stir until these are about to be cooked.
3. Then add cauliflower, cabbage, snow peas, mushrooms and salt to taste.
4. Add a little water for gravy. Stir well till dish is cooked but vegetables are still crisp. Serve.

Note:
Pee hu is available at grocery shops. Imported from China, it is sold in its dried form.

IKAN KUNING
(Turmeric Fish)

600 g chubb mackeral (kembung)
2 pieces dried turmeric (kunyit)
Pepper and salt
Cooking oil

PREPARATION

1. Discard scales, gills and intestines of fish. Clean, drain and pat dry with kitchen paper towels. Cut two to three slits on each side of fish.
2. Pound turmeric finely. Wet with a little water, add 1 tablespoonful salt, a pinch of pepper and mix well. Remove to bowl.
3. Coat fish thoroughly with turmeric mixture. Leave to marinade for 10 – 15 minutes.

METHOD

1. Add oil to heated frying pan. Fry fish. Control heat so that fish does not burn.
2. Turn the fish often to ensure that it does not stick to the pan so that both sides of the fish will be evenly browned when cooked.
3. Serve.

FRESH ANCHOVY FRY OMELETTE

This dish is another which has been snatched from obscurity. However, you may find difficulty in cooking it as fresh anchovy fry and fresh baby shrimps (gerago) are difficult to obtain. Fresh prawns are a good substitute.

100 g fresh baby anchovy (ikan bilis basah)
2 A – sized eggs
1 big red onion
1 fresh red chilli
1 tsp light soya sauce
¼ tsp pepper
8 tbsp cooking oil
1½ tbsp water

PREPARATION

1. Remove heads and intestines of anchovies, wash and drain.
2. Cut onion into rings.
3. Cut chilli into slices at a slant.
4. Beat the eggs in a bowl. Add pepper, light soya sauce, ikan bilis and 1½ tablespoonfuls water. Stir well.

METHOD

1. Heat pan, add oil. When oil is hot, add onion and chilli, fry till soft.
2. Reduce heat to medium, pour in the egg and anchovy mixture.
3. Turn over when the bottom part is cooked, then keep turning until it is nicely browned. Dish out and serve with sambal belacan.

FRIED ANCHOVIES WITH GROUNDNUTS

110 g groundnuts
75 g anchovy (ikan bilis)
4 dried chillies
1 shallot
2 pips garlic
2 tbsp sugar
Salt to taste
Some Indian curry leaves
Cooking oil

PREPARATION

1. Clean anchovies, wash and drain.
2. Soak dried chillies in warm water for 15 minutes then grind finely. Add 1 tablespoonful water to make a sauce.
3. Slice shallots and mince garlic.
4. Wash groundnuts and drain.

METHOD

1. Heat pan, add groundnuts and fry over low heat. Add some salt and stir until water has evaporated. Add 2 tablespoonfuls cooking oil, constantly stirring until groundnuts are brown. Dish out.
2. Wash pan and heat again, add 3 tablespoonfuls of cooking oil till hot, add anchovies, stir until brown and dish out.
3. Fry shallots and garlic, until slightly brown in a table-spoon of heated oil. Add chillies, anchovies, ground-nuts, sugar and Indian curry leaves. Stir to mix well. Serve.

Note:
If there is no oil left after frying ikan bilis, add a tablespoon-ful. Heat the oil before frying onion, garlic and the rest of the ingredients together.

IKAN CENCARU SUMBAT
(Stuffed Hardtail)

4 medium-sized hardtail (cencaru) or horse mackerel

6 shallots, sliced	**(A)**
3 pips garlic	Pounded
2.5 cm shrimp paste (belacan), toasted	finely
2 stalks lemon grass (serai)	

3 fresh red chillies, sliced, deseeded	**(B)**
2 daun limau purut	Pounded
5 dried chillies	finely

Thumb-sized piece turmeric (kunyit), pounded finely
Salt to taste
1 tsp tamarind paste (assam jawa), add 2 tbsp water
Oil for frying

STUFFED HORSE MACKEREL: A standard nyonya way of preparing fish is to stuff them with a sambal before frying.

PREPARATION

1. Pound (A), (B) and turmeric separately. Set aside.
2. In a hot pan, add 1 tablespoonful oil and fry pounded ingredients (A) and (B). Then add 2 tablespoonfuls strained tamarind juice. Set aside.
3. Wash and clean fish. Remove bones. Make 2 horizontal slits along the belly of the fish.
4. Rub fish with salt and turmeric (including inside of slits). Stuff fish well on both sides with pounded fried ingredients.

METHOD

1. Deep fry in hot oil until cooked and golden brown on both sides.
2. Serve hot with rice.

Note:
An alternative method is to sew up the slits after stuffing. Fry fish with slits facing you.

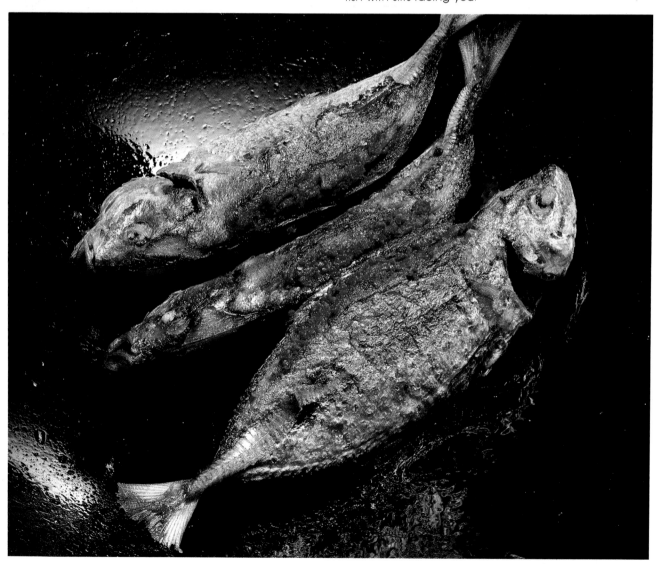

CHINESE POMFRET IN SOYA BEAN SAUCE: Pomfret is a favourite fish, here fried and smoothered with a thick sauce.

FRIED IKAN BAWAL PUTIH WITH TAUCHEONG
(Chinese Pomfret in Soya Bean Sauce)

300 g Chinese pomfret (bawal puteh)
½ big red onion
2 pips garlic
1 piece ginger
1 fresh red chilli
1 tbsp preserved soya bean paste (taucheong)
1 tbsp light soya sauce
Pinch of pepper
Monosodium glutamate/seasoning (optional)
Sprig of spring onion
8 tbsp cooking oil

PREPARATION

1. Clean fish. Wash and drain.
2. Cut onion into quarters.
3. Shred ginger.
4. Mince garlic and slice chillies finely at a slant.
5. Cut spring onion into 5 centimetre lengths.

METHOD

1. Fry fish till brown, dish out and set aside.
2. Using 3 tablespoonfuls of the remaining oil, fry garlic and ginger till soft. Add onions. Stir for 1 minute.
3. Add soya bean paste, stir for another minute, then add 1 rice bowl of water, 1 tablespoonful light soya sauce, chillies, pinch of pepper and seasoning.
4. Simmer, add fish. Boil for 2 minutes and dish out. Serve.

Vegetables

A singular trait of traditional nyonya
vegetable dishes is its liberal use of coconut milk
and pounded roots and spices. Hence dishes in
which different vegetables are simmered in a
rempah result in an unusual rich taste that is
altogether surprising and a discovery to the
uninitiated palate.

The choice of vegetables used in her recipes
says much for the inventiveness of the nyonya
cook and her love for experimentation. She is
not selective about her vegetables; instead she
looked to humble greens that thrived in her
backyard, the kangkong, bayam and even sweet
potato leaves.

The ingenuity and skill of the nyonya cook
was such that she even had her own version of
every vegetarian dish, the masterpiece being the
New Year fare — Jiu Hu Char.

KERANG KUCAI GORENG
(Fried Cockles and Chives)

600 g cockles (kerang)
1 big red onion
2 pips garlic
1 fresh red chilli
4 stalks Chinese chives
5 tbsp cooking oil
Salt to taste
Monosodium glutamate/seasoning (optional)

PREPARATION

1. Wash cockles well, drain and then pour boiling water to cover them and allow to soak for 5 minutes. Remove shells and put cockle flesh into a metal sieve to wash and drain.
2. Cut onion into quarters.
3. Mince garlic.
4. Slice chilli at a slant.
5. Cut Chinese chives into 5 cm lengths.

METHOD

1. Heat pan, add oil, when oil is hot, add onion and minced garlic, stir till soft.
2. Add cockles, chives, chilli, pinch of monosodium glutamate/seasoning and salt to taste.
3. Fry till cockles are just cooked, remove from heat. Serve.

FRIED BRINJALS IN SOYA BEAN PASTE

300 g brinjals
1 tbsp preserved soya bean paste (taucheong)
20 g dried prawns
½ tsp pounded chilli
4 – 5 tbsp oil

PREPARATION

1. Clean brinjals. Cut into 5 – 7 cm lengths. Slice each into two.
2. Soak dried prawns for a few minutes. Drain.

METHOD

1. Heat oil in a frying pan.
2. Add pounded chilli, preserved soya bean paste and dried prawns. Stir till fragrant.
3. Add brinjals. Stir, cover frying pan. Stir now and then until cooked. Serve.

CHAP CHAI LEMAK
(Mixed Vegetables in Coconut milk)

150 g cabbage
6 french beans (optional)
115 g prawns
115 g cauliflower
1 piece soya bean cake (tau kua)
4 pieces fried soya bean cake (tau pok)
30 g transparent vermicelli (tung hoon)
½ coconut, grated
5 tbsp cooking oil
3 fresh red chillies
½ thumb-sized piece turmeric (kunyit)
4 shallots
3 pips garlic

PREPARATION

1. Shred cabbage leaves coarsely.
2. Cut the french beans at a slant into fine pieces.
3. Shell the prawns. Wash, clean and drain.
4. Cut the cauliflower into small pieces.
5. Cut soya bean cake into cubes and fried soya bean cakes into halves.
6. Soak transparent vermicelli until soft.
7. Add 1 rice bowl of water to grated coconut and squeeze for first milk. Add another 2 rice bowls of water to squeeze for second milk.
8. Pound the chillies and turmeric finely. Add shallots and garlic to the pounded ingredients and pound again till fine. Dish out and set aside.

METHOD

1. Heat 3 tablespoonfuls oil in a pot and fry pounded ingredients for a minute.
2. Pour in the second coconut milk and bring to boil.
3. Add prawns, cabbage, french beans, cauliflower and stir for another minute.
4. Add soya bean cake, transparent vermicelli, fried soya bean cake and first coconut milk. Boil for 3 to 5 minutes.
5. Add salt to taste. Stir well for half a minute. Remove and serve.

KERANG KUCAI GORENG: Stir fry the cockles till they are just cooked to retain their natural juices.

FRIED SALT FISH AND TAUGEH

600 g beansprouts (taugeh)
75 g salt fish flesh
1 fresh red chilli
A few stalks Chinese chives
1 tbsp oyster sauce
Monosodium glutamate/seasoning (optional)
3 pips garlic

PREPARATION

1. Wash beansprouts and drain.
2. Clean salt fish and cut into thin slices.
3. Cut chillies into fine slices at a slant.
4. Cut Chinese chives into 5 cm lengths.
5. Fry salt fish until slightly brown and dish out.
6. Mince garlic.

METHOD

1. Heat pan, add 7 tablespoonfuls oil.
2. When oil is hot, add garlic, stir till transparent. Add beansprouts, salt fish, oyster sauce, chillies, pinch of seasoning and pepper to taste.
3. Stir well and add Chinese chives and a little water.
4. Stir till beansprouts are just cooked. Dish out and serve.

FRIED SOYA BEAN CAKE AND LONG BEANS

150 g streaky pork
115 g long beans
75 g dried preserved radish (chai por)
115 g prawns
1 soya bean cake (taukua)
1 big red onion
2 pips garlic
2 fresh red chillies
Monosodium glutamate/seasoning (optional)
7 tbsp cooking oil
Salt to taste

PREPARATION

1. Clean pork and cut into small pieces.
2. Soak dried preserved radish in water for 15 minutes then slice thinly.
3. Shell, wash and drain prawns.
4. Cut onion into quarters.
5. Cut long beans into 5 centimetre lengths.
6. Mince garlic.

METHOD

1. Heat pan. Add 7 tablespoonfuls oil. When oil is hot, fry soya bean cake till brown. Dish out and cut into cubes.
2. Dish out oil leaving about 4 tablespoonfuls. Add garlic and onion. Fry until transparent.
3. Add pork, dried preserved radish and long beans. Stir for 2 minutes. Add a little water and 1 tablespoonful light soya sauce.
4. Simmer until long beans are quite soft. Add prawns, soya bean cake, pinch of seasoning, chillies and salt to taste. Add a little more water if you want some gravy.
5. Stir until all ingredients are cooked. Dish out and serve.

BAYAM MASAK LEMAK
(Spinach in Coconut Milk)

600 g spinach (bayam)
½ coconut, grated
10 shallots
2.5 cm piece shrimp paste (belacan)
2 fresh red chillies
1 tbsp dried prawns
2 cm piece fresh turmeric (kunyit)
2 – 3 tbsp oil for frying

PREPARATION

1. Wash and drain spinach after cutting into 5 cm lengths.
2. Add 1 rice bowl of water to grated coconut and squeeze for first milk. Add another 4 rice bowls of water to the grated coconut and squeeze for second milk. Set aside.
3. Pound chillies, dried prawns, shallots, turmeric and shrimp paste.

METHOD

1. Heat a frying pan. Add oil. When oil is hot, fry pounded ingredients till fragrant.
2. Add in half of the second coconut milk, spinach and salt to taste. Bring to boil. Add in the rest of the second coconut milk. Cover and simmer for about 20 minutes.
3. When spinach is soft enough, pour in first coconut milk. Bring to boil again and turn off heat quickly. Serve.

BEEF FRIED WITH CAULIFLOWER

300 g satay beef
1 big red onion
1 piece ginger
1 fresh red chilli
2 pips garlic
115 g cauliflower
1½ tbsp light soya sauce
3 tbsp oyster sauce
4 tbsp sesame oil
4 tbsp cooking oil
Pinch of salt
Monosodium glutamate/seasoning (optional)

PREPARATION

1. Clean meat and either slice finely or mince coarsely.
2. Cut cauliflower into bite-size pieces.
3. Shred ginger.
4. Cut onion into quarters.
5. Mince garlic and slice chilli finely at a slant.

METHOD

1. Heat pan. Add sesame and cooking oil. When oil is hot add garlic and ginger. Fry till soft.
2. Add meat and light soya sauce. Stir for 3 minutes. Add onion, fry for another two minutes.
3. Add 2 rice bowls of water, oyster sauce, pinch of salt and seasoning. Simmer for 5 minutes and add cauliflower.
4. Fry for 3 more minutes then add chilli.
5. Mix 1 teaspoonful cornflour thoroughly in 2 tablespoonfuls of water, and pour in. Stir quickly and dish out. Serve.

Note:
For those who like to have the beef more tender, simmer the beef on low flame for one hour. Then slice finely before frying. Substitute beef stock for water.

SOTONG FRIED KIN CHAI
(Fried Cuttlefish and Chinese Celery)

300 g cuttlefish
1 big red onion, cut into 4
2 pips garlic, minced
1 stalk Chinese celery (daun salderi/kin chai)
7 tbsp cooking oil
1 tbsp light soya sauce
1 fresh red chilli
Salt to taste

PREPARATION

1. Cut open cuttlefish without breaking the ink sac, otherwise the whole cuttlefish will become coated with the ink. Remove ink sac carefully. Make slits and remove eyes. In the centre of the tentacles is the mouth. Make a small slit and press out the cuttlebone inside. Cut flesh into pieces, clean and drain.
2. Cut onion into quarters and slice off top.
3. Mince garlic and cut Chinese celery into 5 cm lengths.
4. Slice chilli finely.

METHOD

1. Heat frying pan and add oil. Add garlic and onion. Stir for a minute and add cuttlefish, light soya sauce, chilli and salt to taste.
2. Fry till cuttlefish is cooked. If you want some gravy, add some water. Do not overfry or cuttlefish will shrink and harden.
3. Add chilli and Chinese celery. Stir for 1 minute and remove. Serve.

DAUN UBI KELEDEK MASAK LEMAK
(Sweet Potato Leaves in Coconut milk)

600 g sweet potato leaves
75 g dried prawns
4 shallots
2 pips garlic
1 fresh red chilli
1 coconut, grated
Salt to taste

PREPARATION

1. Discard stalks of sweet potato leaves, wash and drain.
2. Clean dried prawns. Wash and drain.
3. Pound chillies, shallots and garlic finely.
4. Add 2½ rice bowls of water to grated coconut and squeeze for milk.

METHOD

1. Pour coconut milk into pot, add dried prawns and pounded ingredients. Stir well. Bring to boil.
2. Add sweet potato leaves and salt to taste. Boil till leaves are soft. Remove quickly from heat. Serve.

JIU HU CHAR WITH SENGKUANG
(Shredded Cuttlefish with Yambean)

Jiu Hu Char is the traditional name for shredded cuttlefish with yambean. Happy reunions on Chinese New Year's Eve are never complete without this dish on the dining table — together with the ubiquitous sambal belacan of course.

1 medium-sized yambean (sengkuang)
150 g cabbage
1 small carrot
300 g streaky pork
3 big red onions
2 pips garlic
75 g dried cuttlefish (The shredded variety can be obtained from certain shops)
9 tbsp cooking oil
Salt to taste
A few stalks spring onions

PREPARATION

1. Shred yambean, cabbage and carrot.
2. Cut pork into bite-size pieces.
3. Cut onions into rings and mince the garlic.
4. Slice the dried cuttlefish finely.
5. Cut spring onions into 3 cm lengths for use as garnish.

METHOD

1. Heat oil in frying pan. Add garlic and onions. Stir till soft and transparent.
2. Add pork and cuttlefish. Stir for 2 minutes before adding yambean and carrot. Stir until these turn soft.
3. Then add cabbage and ½ tablespoon salt to taste. Stir again till all ingredients are cooked. If too dry, add a few tablespoonfuls of water.
4. Remove and garnish with spring onions. Serve.

JIU HU CHAR: A delightful Chinese New Year Salad.

FRIED KANGKONG OR LONG BEANS WITH DRIED PRAWNS

300 g water convolvulus (kangkong) or long beans
4 shallots
3 pips garlic
4 fresh red chillies
20 g dried prawns
¾ tbsp shrimp paste (belacan)
6 tbsp cooking oil

PREPARATION

1. Pluck off leaves of water convolvulus and tender part of stalks. Cut main stalk into 5 centimetre lengths. Wash and drain. For long beans, snip off the two ends and cut into 5 centimetre lengths. Wash and drain.
2. Pound onions, garlic and chillies coarsely.
3. Wash and drain the dried prawns.

METHOD

1. Add oil to heated frying pan. Add pounded ingredients, shrimp paste and dried prawns. Stir until fragrant.
2. Add in water convolvulus stalks first. Fry until just about soft before adding leaves.
3. Fry until vegetable is cooked but slightly crisp.

Note:

This same recipe can be used for lady's fingers. Since it takes longer for lady's fingers to cook, add ½ rice bowl of water and boil longer. Rinse the vegetable clear of slime before cooking and add a little (3 – 4 tablespoonfuls) of tamarind juice when vegetable is about to cook. To prepare, cut off the two ends of the vegetable and slice at a slant into pieces of 1.5 centimetre thickness. The addition of tamarind juice should help absorb any remaining sliminess in the vegetable.

NYONYA CHAP CHAI
(Mixed Vegetables Nyonya Style)

Nyonya Chap Chai like Kiam Chai Arp (Salted Cabbage and Duck Soup) is a traditional dish. Although simple to prepare, it is delicious. This is the nyonya version of the Chinese vegetarian dish.

25 g transparent vermicelli (tung hoon)
20 g dried lily flowers (kim chiam)
A small handful of edible fungus (bok nee)
4 pieces of sweet bean curd strips (teik ga kee)
75 g cabbage
1 small carrot
50 g snow peas
1 piece soya bean cake (tau kua)
1 big red onion
2 pips garlic
1 piece preserved red soya bean (tauju)
5 pieces fried soya bean cake (tau pok)
6 tbsp cooking oil

PREPARATION

1. Cut transparent vermicelli into half or 3 parts and soak in water until soft.
2. Soak dried lily flowers in water till they bloat; snip off tips.
3. Soak edible fungus in water. Drain.
4. Cut sweet bean curd strips into 2.5 centimetre lengths and fry in oil till light brown.
5. Cut cabbage into small pieces, and slice carrot.
6. Fry soya bean cake in oil. Then cut into eights and slice each into two horizontally.
7. Cut onion into quarters and slice off the heads. Mince the garlic.
8. Cut fried soya bean cake into quarters.

METHOD

1. Heat frying pan. Add oil and minced garlic. Stir for a minute and add sliced onion.
2. Stir for another minute and add preserved red soya bean and a little water to dissolve it. Add cabbage, carrot, edible fungus, dried lotus flowers and snow peas.
3. Stir for 1½ minutes. Add some water to make a little gravy. Stir.
4. Add fried soya bean cakes, bean curd strips, soya bean cake, transparent vermicelli, pepper and salt to taste.
5. Stir carefully until ingredients are soft and cooked, and gravy is bubbling.
6. Remove from heat and serve.

Note:

The tips of onion heads have to be sliced off when onions are quartered so that each quarter will open up into individual layers during cooking.

(OVERLEAF) NYONYA CHAP CHAI: The vegetables provide the sweetness and the preserved red soya bean paste the saltiness in this mixed vegetable dish which is fortified with a variety of soya bean products and edible fungi.

KOBIS MASAK LEMAK (1)
(Cabbage in Coconut Milk)

225 g cabbage
1 small carrot
1 small red sweet potato
4 fresh red chillies
1 big onion
50 – 75 g dried prawns
Thumb-sized piece shrimp paste (belacan)
½ coconut, grated
3 tbsp cooking oil
Salt to taste
2 pips garlic

PREPARATION

1. Cut cabbage into bite-size pieces. Wash and drain.
2. Cut carrot into decorative shapes.
3. Cut sweet potatoes into small pieces.
4. Pound chillies, shallots and garlic till fairly fine.
5. Wash dried prawns and drain.
6. Add 2 rice bowls of water to the grated coconut and squeeze for milk.

METHOD

1. Heat pot. Add cooking oil. When hot, fry pounded ingredients, shrimp paste and dried prawns.
2. Stir well for ½ to 1 minute. Add about 2 rice bowls of water, before adding sweet potatoes and carrots. Boil until carrots and sweet potatoes are cooked.
3. Add coconut milk, cabbage and salt to taste. Bring to boil.
4. When vegetables are cooked, serve.

Note:
If you do not particularly like cabbage, you could substitute it with spinach or sweet potato leaves.

KOBIS MASAK LEMAK (2)
(Cabbage in Coconut Milk)

250 – 300 g cabbage
200 – 250 g fresh prawns
½ coconut, grated
5 fresh red chillies
5 – 6 shallots
1 cm piece shrimp paste (belacan)
1 cm piece fresh young turmeric (kunyit)
Salt to taste
Monosodium glutamate/seasoning (optional)

PREPARATION

1. Cut cabbage into bite-size pieces. Wash and drain.
2. Wash, shell and clean fresh prawns.
3. Add ½ rice bowl of water to grated coconut and squeeze for first milk. Add another 2 rice bowls of water and squeeze for second coconut milk.
4. Grind chillies, shallots, shrimp paste and fresh young turmeric finely.

METHOD

1. Put second coconut milk with ground ingredients in a pot. Bring to a boil.
2. Add cabbage.
3. When nearly cooked, add prawns.
4. Continue simmering for 3 – 5 minutes till prawns are nearly cooked. Add first coconut milk, salt to taste and finally seasoning. Serve.

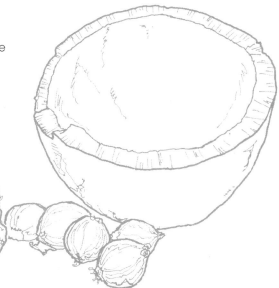

KERABU TAUGEH
(Beansprout Salad Nyonya Style)

300 g beansprouts
½ rice bowl grated coconut
150 g prawns
40 g dried prawns
4 fresh red chillies
1 tsp shrimp paste, toasted
3 shallots
1 big lime

PREPARATION

1. Soak the beansprouts in water, wash and drain. Put into a container or pot of boiling water to scald for half a minute or so. Remove quickly so that it will retain its crispness.
2. Fry grated coconut in pan till it is brown. Pound finely.
3. Soak the dried prawns. Clean, drain and pound coarsely.
4. Pound the chillies finely, together with toasted shrimp paste.
5. Cut shallots into thin slices and cut the lime into fours.
6. Peel prawns, wash and drain. Fry prawns in 1 table-spoonful oil till cooked. Slice into two.

METHOD

1. Squeeze lime juice into pounded shrimp paste and chillies. Mix well.
2. Put beansprouts into a big bowl. Add pounded chillies, dried prawns, fried prawns, fried grated coconut and sliced shallots. Mix well with (1). Adjust ingredients according to personal taste. Serve.

Note:
Kerabu is a mixture of cold ingredients.

EGG AND CUCUMBER KERABU

1½ cucumbers
2 eggs, hardboiled
150 g fresh prawns
150 g dried prawns
55 g edible fungus (bok nee)
2 tsp shrimp paste (belacan)
½ tbsp phaeomaria (bunga kantan)
½ bowl lime juice
Sugar and salt to taste

PREPARATION

1. Cut cucumber into quarters, remove core and dice.
2. Dice hardboiled eggs.
3. Cut edible fungus into 2 centimetre squares.
4. Slice phaeomaria finely.
5. Wash and drain dried prawns, pound coarsely.
6. Shell fresh prawns, devein, wash and steam.

METHOD

1. Combine lime juice, shrimp paste, dried prawns and phaeomaria in a bowl.
2. Add cucumber, eggs, fresh prawns and edible fungus. Mix well.
3. Add sugar and salt to taste. Serve.

Noodles & Rice

Variety is the essence of Northern nyonya noodle and rice dishes. In preparation, flavour, texture and colour, there are subtle and interesting differences. Fine examples can be experienced in Nasi Ulam, Kerabu Meehoon, Penang Assam Laksa and Nyonya Prawn Congee.
Nasi Ulam uses a variety of subtle aromatic leaves which used to thrive in every nyonya family's backyard — daun kaduk, daun limau purut, daun kesom, daun cekur, to name a few. Kerabu Meehoon is an inviting concoction of rice vermicelli, grated coconut, fried soya bean cake, beansprouts, sliced onions and hard boiled eggs served with the indispensible sambal belacan. As for Penang Assam Laksa, this dish (more a meal) is in a class of its own. Its rich spicy and fragrant gravy, garnished with flavouring leaves of mint and kesum and topped generously with prawn paste is a taste sensation very different from the Southern nyonya version which has beansprouts, fish cakes, cockles and prawns. Nyonya Congee is a very special tasty breakfast or supper treat. Of these, Prawn Congee is an old favourite.

NASI MINYAK

1½ heaped rice bowls rice
3 level tbsp Q.B.B. ghee and 3 tbsp margarine
35 – 40 raisins
75 g cashew nuts
½ small tin tomato juice or 3 tbsp tomato sauce
4 cloves (bunga cengkih)
110 g ginger
5 cm cinnamon sticks (kayu manis)
2 star anise (bunga lawang)
2 shallots
2 pips garlic

PREPARATION

1. Pound ginger finely and squeeze for juice.
2. Wash rice and drain well.
3. Slice shallots and mince garlic.

METHOD

1. Heat pan, add ghee and margarine.
2. When oil is hot, add onions, garlic, cinnamon sticks, cloves and star anise. Stir till fragrant. Add cashew nuts and raisins. Stir a few times.
3. Add rice and stir well to mix ingredients.
4. Dish out mixture and put into rice cooker, add ginger juice and tomato juice, pinch of salt, then add water to cook rice.
5. Stir rice during cooking. When cooked, serve with meat or chicken curry.

SIAMESE LAKSA

600 g fresh coarse rice vermicelli
600 g hardtail (cencaru)
1 coconut, grated

2 stalks lemon grass (serai), sliced finely
Thumb-sized piece fresh young
    turmeric (kunyit)   (A)
6 dried chillies, soaked in warm   Pounded finely
    water for 15 minutes
4 fresh red chillies, sliced

5 shallots
                          (B) Pounded finely
4 pips garlic

½ tsp shrimp paste (belacan)
2 pieces tamarind (assam keping)
4 young daun limau purut, do not use old leaves
1 thumb-sized piece galangal (lengkuas), bruised
10 tbsp cooking oil

GARNISH INGREDIENTS
1 cucumber, remove skin and pith. Shredded
1 small pineapple, skinned, remove eyes, washed, shredded
2 bundles mint leaves (daun pudina), discard stalk,
1 phaeomaria (bunga kantan), minced
1 big red onion, cut into rings
2 – 3 fresh red chillies, discard seeds, Sliced finely
Black prawn paste (heh koh)
To serve, put coarse vermicelli into a bowl. Garnish, add gravy. Add prawn paste to taste.

PREPARATION

1. Add 1 rice bowl of water to grated coconut and squeeze for first milk. Add another rice bowl of water and squeeze for second milk. Set aside.
2. Stir coarse rice vermicelli in a pot of boiling water till soft but not too limp. Remove and drain.
3. Remove scales and intestines of fish. Wash, clean and pat dry with kitchen paper towels.
4. Pound ingredients (A) and (B) separately.

METHOD

1. Heat oil in cooking pot on a medium flame. When hot, add pounded ingredients and shrimp paste. Stir for a minute and reduce heat to medium.
2. Add the second coconut milk carefully to the mixture in the pot. Stir well till fragrant. The ingredients should be bubbling in the oil. If it is too dry, add a teaspoonful or two of oil.
3. Pour in remaining second coconut milk, then add fish, daun limau purut, galangal and tamarind. Increase heat, add salt to taste and boil mixture for 2 – 3 minutes.
4. Add all of the first coconut milk. Reduce heat and allow mixture to slow boil for 5 minutes. Set aside.

Note:
Do not over soak the fresh coarse rice vermicelli as it is already cooked when bought. Oversoaking will result in soggy vermicelli. If you are using a metal pot, control of heat is very important as oil gets hot very fast. If your stirring is too slow, your ingredients will burn and get stuck to the bottom of the pot. Shrimp paste is a very important part of this recipe so make sure you use a good quality one.

It is advisable that coconut milk is added bit by bit while you are stirring the mixture in the pot. This will prevent your mixture from drying up.

NYONYA CHICKEN PORRIDGE

½ chicken
¾ heaped rice bowl rice, washed and drained
75 g ginger, shredded
1 stalk coriander leaves (daun ketumbar)
Pepper
Sesame oil

METHOD

1. Debone and shred chicken.
2. Put the chicken bones in a pot and add 2½ rice bowls of water. Boil for 15 to 20 minutes. Remove bones and cool the chicken stock.
3. Add rice and chicken flesh into stock and heat again. Boil until rice grains break open. The porridge should be just watery. If not, add some water.
4. Add ½ teaspoon salt and bring to boil again. Remove from heat.
5. To serve, scoop porridge into a bowl, add some shredded ginger, coriander leaves, a shake of pepper and a few drops sesame oil.

MEE REBUS

300 g fresh yellow noodles
150 g beansprouts (taugeh)

40 g prawns, shelled and cleaned
3 tbsp Indian beans (parapu)
150 g sweet potato   (A)

150 g prawns shelled, cleaned and minced finely
100 g flour sieved
1 small egg
½ tsp salt
½ level tsp baking powder
3 tbsp cooking oil

PREPARATION FOR GRAVY

1. Soak noodles in boiling water for 1 minute. Drain and set aside.
2. Remove beansprouts ends. Drain and wash. Scald in boiling water briefly to retain crispness. Drain and set aside.
3. Soak Indian beans in water for 20 minutes. Clean, drain.
4. Boil sweet potato and Indian beans in about 1 rice bowl of water till soft.
5. Blend (A) together in an electric blender using about 1 rice bowl of water. The result should be about 1½ rice bowls of gravy.

METHOD: GRAVY

1. Put blended ingredients of (A) into a pot. Add 1 tablespoonful sugar, ½ teaspoon salt and 3 table-spoonfuls cooking oil. Bring to slow boil for 10 minutes. The gravy should be of nice medium thick consistency.

GARNISHING

1. 2 pieces soya bean cake. Fry in oil till brown. Remove. Cool. Cut each piece into eight.
2. 2 hard boiled eggs. Shell, cut into eight.
3. 10 shallots. Remove skin, cut into fine slices. Deep fry with a little salt until light brown or transparent. Quickly dish out.
4. 1 red and green chilli. Slice finely. Remove seeds. Set aside.

PRAWN FRITTERS

1. Put minced prawns into a bowl. Add flour, egg, baking powder and salt. Stir slowly until batter is well mixed.
2. Add water bit by bit until smooth soft batter is obtained.
3. Deep fry in hot oil a spoonful at a time till fritter is brown and cooked. Remove, drain and use kitchen paper towels to absorb any excess oil.
4. Cut into bite-sized pieces. Set aside.

Note:
To make good prawn fritters, the consistency of the batter must neither be too thin nor too thick. When scooped into a spoon and allowed to dribble, it should flow like a thick cream.

CHILLI SAUCE

1. 6 dried chillies. Soak in warm water for 15 minutes. Drain and pound finely.
2. 4 shallots. Slice finely. Add to pounded chillies and pound till fine again.
3. 3 pips garlic. Mince. Add to (2) and pound finely.

METHOD

1. Heat pan, add 6 tablespoonfuls oil. When oil is hot, add pounded ingredients. Slow fry for 2 minutes.
2. Add 2 tablespoonfuls water and ¼ teaspoon salt. Stir well till it boils in the oil. Dish out.
3. To serve Mee Rebus, put sufficient noodles into a deep plate or serving bowl.
4. Garnish with soya bean cake, prawn fritters, eggs, red and green sliced chillies, shallots and a little chilli sauce. Add gravy and serve.

NASI KUNYIT

600 g glutinous rice
1 coconut, grated
2 pieces thumb-sized turmeric (kunyit)
2 pieces tamarind (assam keping)
8 screwpine leaves (daun pandan)
1½ rice bowls water
½ tsp salt
30 white peppercorns

PREPARATION

1. Pound turmeric finely.
2. Wash glutinous rice and drain.
3. Put glutinous rice into a deep container. Add water till rice is covered. Put the pounded turmeric into a metal sieve or coffee strainer. Dip it into the soaked rice. Stir slowly till rice and water become evenly yellow. Allow the rice to soak for 5 to 6 hours.
4. Add 1½ rice bowls of water to grated coconut and squeeze for milk. Set aside.

METHOD

1. Drain the glutinous rice.
2. Place screwpine leaves on the steaming tray and spread the glutinous rice on top. Steam for 20 minutes.
3. Remove glutinous rice and place in a container. Add ½ teaspoon salt to the coconut milk and stir well, then pour the coconut milk into the steamed glutinous rice. Stir the rice to mix well with the coconut milk.
4. Place another 4 screwpine leaves on the steaming tray and spread the steamed glutinous rice on top. Steam for another 20 minutes. Remove and serve with nasi kunyit curry. (See page 43)

PENANG ASSAM LAKSA

600 g fresh coarse rice vermicelli
600 g chubb mackeral (kembung)

5 shallots
2 stalks lemon grass (serai), sliced finely
Thumb-sized piece fresh young
    turmeric (kunyit)
7 dried chillies, soaked in warm
    water for 15 minutes
3 fresh red chillies (omit this if you want
    a less hot gravy)

(A)
Ground finely

5 cm piece shrimp paste (belacan)
5 rice bowls water
2 pieces tamarind (assam keping)
1 tsp sugar
1 phaeomaria (bungan kantan)

1 cucumber
5 – 6 stalks polygonum (daun kesum)
1 bundle mint leaves (daun pudina)
2 big red onions, cut into rings
3 fresh red chillies, sliced finely as a slant
1 small pineapple

For garnishing

Monosodium glutamate/seasoning (optional)
Black prawn paste (heh koh)

PREPARATION

1. Skin cucumber, slice, discard core and shred.
2. Scoop a few tablespoonfuls of prawn paste into a bowl. Dissolve in a little warm water.
3. Skin pineapple, cut off eyes, wash and shred.
4. Prepare ground ingredients (A).

METHOD

1. Stir fresh coarse rice vermicelli in hot water for a few minutes after separating and rinsing under cold water. Remove and drain.
2. Into a pot, add 2 rice bowls of water. Add fish. Boil until cooked. Remove fish. Discard bones (alternately, steam fish and flake).
3. Add another rice bowl of water to pot. Put in ground ingredients (A).
4. Boil till gravy is fragrant. Add fish flesh, sugar and salt to taste. Check to ensure that shrimp paste dissolves. Boil gravy for 10 – 15 minutes at low heat.
5. To serve, put coarse vermicelli into a bowl. Garnish with pineapple, cucumber, chillies, mint leaves and onions. Add gravy. Add prawn paste according to personal taste.

Note:
An excellent substitute for chubb mackeral is wolf herring (parang). It gives a sweeter, tastier gravy. A can of sardines is also a good substitute if fresh fish is not readily available. See note on Siamese Laksa.

PENANG ASSAM LAKSA: The epitome of northern nyonya cooking.

HOKKIEN MEE

300 g fresh yellow noodles
180 g rice vermicelli
225 g beansprouts (taugeh)
225 g water convolvulus (kangkong)
300 g prawns
300 g pork bones
225 g lard
Light soya sauce
15 shallots
5 tbsp cooking oil
10 dried chillies, soaked in warm water for 15 minutes
4 pips garlic

PREPARATION

1. Soak noodles in boiling water for 1 minute. Dish out and drain.
2. Soak rice vermicelli in water till soft.
3. Clean beansprouts and drain. Scald in boiling water till cooked but still crispy. Set aside.
4. Snip off water convolvulus leaves and young parts of stem. Wash, drain. Scald in boiling water. Set aside.
5. Shell prawns, wash and drain. Keep heads and shells.
6. Wash and drain lard. Cube.
7. Slice shallots finely. Deep fry till transparent. Set aside.
8. Grind or pound chillies. Add shallots and garlic to the pounded ingredients and pound again till fine. Set aside.

METHOD

1. Fry cubed lard in heated kuali. Stir at medium heat till lard produces oil. When cubes have shrunk and turned brown, dish into small bowl together with oil. Set aside.
2. In a heated kuali, add 8 tablespoonfuls of oil. Add pounded ingredients, ½ tablespoon salt, 3 table-spoonfuls water. Stir at medium heat until fragrant. If it dries too fast, add a teaspoonful or so of water and stir until chilli mixture has a medium consistency. Dish out and set aside.
3. Pound prawn heads and shells coarsely. Fill a pot with 1½ rice bowls of water. Add pork bones, slow boil for ½ an hour.
4. Dish out pork bones, add pounded shells and prawns heads and slow boil for another 10 minutes.
5. Meanwhile remove meat from pork bones. Turn off heat, pour gravy into a container through a strainer or sieve.
6. Clean pot, pour strained gravy back, add pork, prawns and simmer for 10 – 15 minutes. Add salt to taste. The gravy is now ready for serving.
7. To serve, put noodles, rice vermicelli, beansprouts and water convolvulus into a bowl. Add gravy mixture and garnish with pork oil, lard crusts, fried shallots slices and some light soya sauce and chilli sauce.

NYONYA PRAWN PORRIDGE

½ heaped rice bowl rice
300 g prawns, shelled, washed, drained
2 tbsp light soya sauce
10 pips garlic, minced coarsely
½ tsp salt
Monosodium glutamate/seasoning (optional)
Pepper
300 g groundnuts
Cooking oil
A pinch of preserved radish
1 stalk Chinese celery (daun salderi)

PREPARATION

1. Clean groundnuts and drain. It must be fried im-mediately to prevent it from getting soggy and losing its crispness. Put into pan, over low heat, stirring continuously until water dries up. Then add 3 table-spoonfuls oil, 1 teaspoonful salt and keep stirring until groundnuts are brown. Dish out and cool.
2. Wash Chinese celery and cut into small pieces. Set aside.
3. Fry 8 pips minced garlic with 7 tablespoonfuls oil till brown. Set aside.

METHOD

1. Heat pan, add 4 tablespoonfuls oil till hot. Add 2 pips minced garlic, stir till soft, add prawns and ¼ tea-spoon salt. Stir until prawns are cooked. Dish out and set aside.
2. Wash rice and drain, put into pot, add 2 rice bowls of water. Boil rice until rice grains break open. Add fried prawns, preserved radish, 2 tablespoonfuls light soya sauce. The porridge at this stage should be just watery, if not add some water. Stir well to mix the ingredients. Bring to boil and remove heat. Do not cover pot or porridge will become too thick.
3. To serve, scoop porridge into bowl, add a teaspoonful fried garlic, shake in some pepper and garnish with Chinese celery. Serve with fried groundnuts.

NYONYA FRIED RICE

1 plate of freshly cooked or overnight rice
1 tbsp dried prawns
1 A-Sized egg
2 fresh red chillies
2 cm square shrimp paste (belacan)
2 shallots
2 pips garlic, minced
1 tsp light soya sauce
½ tsp dark soya sauce
1 sprig spring onion
3 tbsp sesame oil
3 tbsp cooking oil
Monosodium glutamate/seasoning

PREPARATION

1. Wash and drain dried prawns after soaking in a little water for one minute. Pound coarsely.
2. Pound chillies till fine then shallots and garlic. Mix well. Dish out.
3. Slice spring onions finely.

METHOD

1. Heat frying pan. Add 3 tablespoonfuls sesame oil.
2. When oil is hot, add sliced onions and minced garlic. Reduce heat and add pounded chillies, dried prawns and stir for half a minute till fragrant. Then add shrimp paste. Stir till shrimp paste dissolves.
3. Add rice and dark and light soya sauces. Stir until ingredients are well mixed. Push the rice to the edge of the frying pan.
4. Add 3 tablespoonfuls oil to frying pan. When oil is hot, crack in the egg. Cover egg with fried rice when the bottom of the egg is slightly cooked. Fry mixture till egg is fully cooked. Add spring onion. Stir. Add salt and pepper to taste.

Note:

For those who prefer a 'heavier' meal, add roasted pork, fresh prawns or chicken meat. Cube these first. If rice is freshly cooked, cool first or rice will stick together during frying. If rice has a sticky consistency, stir until it is dry.

KERABU MEE HOON

300 g rice vermicelli
¼ coconut, grated
A handful of beansprouts (taugeh)
300 g prawns
2 eggs
2 pieces soya bean cake (taukua)
6 shallots
3 big limes
Some coriander leaves

PREPARATION

1. Soak rice vermicelli in water until soft. Remove and drain. Cook in boiling water for 1 minute. Dish out and drain.
2. Scald beansprouts in the same boiling water till cooked but crisp, dish out and drain.
3. Hard boil eggs. Shell and cut into slices.
4. Cut soya bean cakes into short lengths and deep fry till brown. Dish out and set aside.
5. Fry grated coconut (without oil or water) till brown. Dish out and pound finely.
6. Shell prawns, wash and drain. Slow fry with a little salt until cooked (no oil is needed). Dish out, cool and slice into halves.
7. Cut some coriander leaves and set aside.
8. Cut limes into halves.
9. Slice shallots finely.

METHOD

1. Put boiled rice vermicelli and beansprouts into a big plate, add fried soya bean cake, and fried coconut. Mix well.
2. Add 1½ tablespoonfuls water to rice vermicelli mixture for some gravy.
3. Put sliced shallots into a bowl and add a little salt. Mix well, add into rice vermicelli.
4. Add lime juice to rice vermicelli and mix well. Add salt and pepper to taste.
5. Garnish with eggs, fried prawns, coriander leaves, sliced chillies (optional) and serve with sambal belacan.

NASI LEMAK: Coconut flavoured rice served here with a trio of simple sambals.

NASI LEMAK

At it's simplest, nasi lemak is a snack served with a few slices of cucumber, a sprinkling of ikan bilis and a dob of sambal belacan. Accompanied by other dishes like curry, egg sambal, fried water convolvulus or udang assam goreng it becomes a feast befitting any occasion.

1 heaped rice bowl rice
½ coconut, grated
3 screwpine leaves (daun pandan)

PREPARATION

1. Add 1 rice bowl of water to grated coconut to squeeze for milk.
2. Wash rice and drain.
3. Wash screwpine leaves, slit into two from the middle and knot.

METHOD

1. Put rice into rice cooker, add coconut milk and water till the level of liquid is about a centimetre above the rice.
2. Add screwpine leaves and bring to boil, stirring once a while with a pair of chopsticks.
3. When rice is about to dry up cover pot and simmer until cooked.
4. Serve with a selection of sambals. (See section on Sambals).

NASI ULAM/NASI KERABU

Nasi ulam is a dish that uses generous amounts of fresh herbs and is served cold. In the old days, making this dish was easy as pie since herbs were plentiful in one's backyard. Aside from daun pandan, daun limau purut and serai, there were always mint leaves (daun pudina) sweet potato leaves, daun kaduk, daun kesum, daun cekur as well as banana leaves. A good part of these fresh herbs is used in the preparation of nasi ulam.

Cooked rice
A bunch of daun kaduk
150 g salt fish flesh
8 cekur leaves
5 daun limau purut
½ young coconut, grated
Pepper and salt to taste

NASI ULAM: Daun limau purut at rear, cekur leaf in front and daun kaduk on the right — all blended together with grated coconut to make a sensational rice dish.

PREPARATION

1. Wash and clean the daun kaduk, daun cekur and daun limau purut. Shred them separately and place in a plate.
2. Fry the grated coconut (without oil or water) at low heat till brown. Cool and pound finely.
3. Toast the salt fish over low heat till brown. Remove and shred.

METHOD

1. To 1 plate hot rice, add the shredded daun kaduk, daun cekur and daun limau purut in the following proportions: 4:2:1.
2. Add some salt fish, fried coconut, pepper and salt to taste.
3. Mix well and serve.

INDIAN MEE/KUIH TEOW GORENG
(Indian Fried Noodles)

300 g fresh yellow noodles or flat rice noodles
125 g beansprouts (taugeh)
2 pieces soya bean cake (taukua)
2 small potatoes
1 hard boiled egg
5 dried chillies
4 pips garlic, minced
1 big lime
¾ tsp tamarind paste (assam jawa)
Sugar and salt to taste
7 tbsp cooking oil
1 tbsp light soya sauce
Dark soya sauce to taste
6 shallots
1 red and 1 green chilli
Some spring onion, sliced
150 g prawns
90 g flour, sieved
½ level tsp baking powder
1 C-sized egg
1 level tbsp sugar

PREPARATION

1. Put noodles into a metal sieve and pour in boiling water to scald. Alternately, plunge into boiling water and drain.
2. Remove beansprout ends. Wash well and drain. Scald briefly in boiling water to cook and retain crispness.
3. Fry soya bean cake till brown and cut into eight.
4. Add a little water to tamarind paste and strain for 5 tablespoonfuls juice.
5. Skin potatoes and cut into bite-size pieces.
6. Shell hard boiled egg and cut into slices or eights.
7. Soak dried chillies in warm water for 10 minutes. Drain well and pound finely. Add 2 tablespoonfuls water and mix well. Set aside.
8. Skin shallots, slice finely and fry in oil and a little salt. When brown and transparent, remove.
9. Slice red and green chillies finely after removing seeds.

PRAWN FRITTERS

1. Shell, clean and drain prawns. Mince finely. Put into a bowl and add flour that has been sieved, and ½ level teaspoon baking powder.
2. Break in egg and slowly stir until egg is well mixed with flour and other ingredients.
3. Add water little by little till a batter of smooth liquid consistency is achieved. (See note in Mee Rebus).
4. Deep fry spoonfuls in hot oil. Drain and cut into bite-size pieces. Set aside.

METHOD

1. Heat frying pan, add 5 tablespoonfuls oil. When hot add minced garlic.
2. Stir for ten seconds, add noodles by the handful. Add beansprouts, pounded dried chillies, a tablespoonful or two of tamarind juice, 1 tablespoonful light soya sauce, a few drops dark soya sauce and salt and sugar to taste.
3. Quickly add prawn fritters, soya bean cake and potato slices. Stir well until cooked.
4. Remove to dish and garnish with egg slices, sliced spring onions, sliced chillies and shallots.
5. Squeeze some lime juice from lime pieces on the noodles before serving.

Note:
The addition of salt to sliced shallots when frying is to keep shallots crisp. If you want your dish to be more sour, add extra tamarind juice.

BIRTHDAY MEE

300 g yellow egg noodles
300 g fairly big prawns
150 g chicken meat
75 g crab meat
200 g streaky pork
115 g beansprouts (taugeh)
2 big eggs
2 stalks of coriander leaves (daun ketumbar)
1 fresh red chilli
5 tbsp oil

PREPARATION

1. Scald noodles in boiling water for half a minute and drain.
2. Shell prawns, clean, wash and drain.
3. Shred chicken meat.
4. Remove beansprout ends. Clean, drain and scald in boiling water till cooked but still crispy.
5. Clean coriander leaves and break into several pieces.
6. Remove chilli seeds and slice chilli finely.

METHOD

1. Beat eggs. Heat pan, add 5 tablespoonfuls oil. Pour in eggs.
2. Hold the two ears of the pan with a cloth, lift pan up and swirl to spread egg thinly. Turn egg over when cooked and slightly brown. Remove. Shred. Set aside.
3. Fill a pot with 6 rice bowls water. Bring to the boil and add pork. When it is nearly cooked, remove pork, slice away skin and shred meat. Bring liquid in the pot to a boil again.
4. Add chicken meat, prawns, shredded pork, crab meat. Slow boil until ingredients are cooked. Remove heat. To serve, put noodles and beansprouts into a deep plate. Pour gravy mixture over. Garnish with sliced eggs, chilli, coriander leaves and sambal belacan.

BIRTHDAY MEE: What a wonderful breakfast to wake up to on one's birthday.

Soups

Soups do not feature predominantly in nyonya cuisine. Unlike staples like gulais and sambals that crown the family table at mealtimes, soups are included only occasionally. Yet they are not inconsequential but rather like limited editions to be enjoyed leisurely. For aside from the simple and homely soups such as Bayam th'ng (spinach soup), soups are musts on festive occasions. Much ado is made about its cooking and only choice ingredients go into its preparation. Kiam Chai Arp, Poh Ho Th'ng and Hu Peow Th'ng are such soups — all unique and wonderful.

PAU HU TH'NG
(Abalone Soup)

1 tin abalone
150 g pork
225 g ginko nuts (pak kor)
3 pieces soya bean strips (fu chok)
1 small carrot
30 – 35 g mushrooms, soaked in water
Monosodium glutamate/seasoning (optional)
Salt to taste

PREPARATION

1. Shell and soak ginko nuts in water for ½ an hour. Remove skin and clean.
2. Cut abalone into slices.
3. Cut pork into pieces.
4. Cut soya bean strips into 6 centimetre lengths. Soak in water for 5 minutes.
5. Skin carrot, slice and cut into decorative shapes.
6. Cut mushrooms into two.

METHOD

1. Fill pot with 3½ rice bowls of water, add pork and carrots, bring to boil. Add ginko nuts, slow boil till all three ingredients are cooked.
2. Add abalone, mushroom, soya bean strips, a little seasoning and salt to taste. Boil for 5 minutes and remove from heat and serve.

Note:
Ginko nuts are available from Chinese medical halls or big grocery shops.

PAU HU TH'NG: The delicacy which is abalone makes this soup popular at parties.

KIAM CHAI ARP: Nutmeg seeds, red coloured kei chee and sour plums lend their subtle flavour to this nyonya standard.

KIAM CHAI ARP
(Duck in Salted Mustard Soup)

1 duck about 1¼ kg in weight
500 g local or China salted mustard greens (kiam chai)
2 wet sour plum (suin muei) OR 2 pieces tamarind
   (assam keping)
5 fresh red chillies
2 nutmeg seeds
30 white peppercorns
20 – 30 kei chee

PREPARATION

1. Cut the duck into pieces. Clean and drain.
2. Cut the salted mustard greens into 5 cm lengths. Clean and drain.
3. Make a slit and remove seeds of chillies (do not slice open completely).
4. Crack the nutmeg shell to remove seeds.

METHOD

1. Fill a pot with 4 – 5 rice bowls of water. Bring to boil and add salted mustard greens. Slow boil the salted mustard greens with pot covered until it is half cooked.
2. Add duck, pepper, tamarind pieces OR sourplums, nutmeg seeds and chillies. Check water level, top up till it covers ingredients.
3. Cover pot and slow boil till duck and kiam chai are soft. Simmer for ½ an hour.
4. Serve.

Note:
A good guide to amount of water to start with would be to use the ratio of 2:1 of water to salted mustard greens. While soup is boiling, taste for saltiness. Either add water if it is too salty or remove tamarind pieces. If left too long in the soup, it will make the soup too sour.

* Sour plum, nutmeg seeds and kei chee can be obtained from larger sundry shops or Chinese medical halls.
* Local salted mustard greens give a better taste in this dish but takes a longer time than China salted mustard greens to soften.

SENGKUANG KOON TH'NG
(Yambean Soup)

200 g yambean (sengkuang), skinned
300 g pork bones
75 g dried cuttlefish (sotong)
10 white peppercorns
2 rice bowls water
Salt

PREPARATION

1. Clean yambean and cut into 2.5 centimetre squares. Cut each square into 3 pieces.
2. Chop up pork bone and soak dried cuttlefish. Cut cuttlefish into same size as yambean.
3. Pound peppercorns till they break open.

METHOD

1. Boil water in a pot.
2. Add all ingredients and bring to boil again.
3. Simmer until ingredients are cooked and soft enough. Add extra water if soup is insufficient.
4. Add salt to taste. Serve.

Note:
If you find that peppercorns make this dish too hot for your taste, use pepper powder instead. No soya sauce is to be added to the soup.

SALT FISH SOYA BEAN SOUP

300 g salt fish bones
5 pieces soft soya bean cake (tauhu)
150 g lean pork with some fat
200 g prawns
5 slices ginger
5 pips garlic, sliced

PREPARATION

1. Clean and soak fish bones in 3½ rice bowls of water. Retain water.
2. Cut soft soya bean cakes into quarters.
3. Cut pork into bite-size cubes.
4. Shell prawns, clean and wash.

METHOD

1. Put oil into heated cooking pot. Add garlic and ginger. Stir till slightly brown.

2. Add pork, stir for 1 – 2 minutes. Slowly pour in the salt fish water, then the salt fish bones. Bring to boil.
3. Add soft soya bean cakes and prawns. Cover pot, reduce heat and slow boil for 10 minutes. Serve.

Note:
No salt is required as the salt fish water is already salty. If you find that the salt fish water is too salty for your personal taste, discard some and substitute equal amount of plain water. Slow boiling this dish is to prevent evaporation of the soup and to bring out its taste and fragrance.

TRANSPARENT VERMICELLI AND FISH BALL SOUP

12 medium sized fish balls
40 g transparent vermicelli (tung hoon)
1½ tsp preserved radish (tung chai)
1 shallot, sliced finely
Pepper
2 pips garlic, minced
Salt to taste
2 tbsp cooking oil
Chinese cruellers (yu char kway)

PREPARATION

1. Cut transparent vermicelli into 10 centimetre lengths and soak in water for 5 minutes.
2. Fry minced garlic in 2 tablespoonfuls oil.

METHOD

1. Boil 3 rice bowls of water in a pot. Add transparent vermicelli, preserved radish and salt to taste.
2. Boil transparent vermicelli till soft, then add fish balls. Boil again for 2 – 3 minutes and quickly remove from heat. If not fish balls will shrink and harden.
3. Serve garnished with shallots, a little pepper and fried garlic.
4. Serve with Chinese cruellers cut into bite-size pieces.

HU PEOW PIG'S INTESTINE SOUP
(Dried Fish Floating Bladder and Intestine Soup)

Hu Peow is dried fish floating bladder which is available at provision shops or Chinese medical halls. Normally eaten on the 15th day of the Chinese New Year (Chap Goh Meh), Hu Peow soup is a delicious blend of any number of choice ingredients: mushrooms, chicken flesh, pork, prawns, fish balls. A real hearty soup if there was any. There are two popular ways in which this delicacy is often prepared.

75 g dried fish floating bladder (hu peow)
200 g pork intestines
150 g pork
115 g groundnuts
15 white peppercorns
1 big red onion
Monosodium glutamate/seasoning (optional)
Salt to taste

PREPARATION

1. Wash and clean the intestines.
2. Soak dried floating bladder until soft and cut into pieces.
3. Cut pork into pieces.
4. Soak groundnuts in hot water for ½ an hour after adding ½ teaspoon salt. Peel off skin (salt facilitates easy peeling).
5. Cut onions into quarters.

METHOD

1. Heat pot, add 2 rice bowls of water and intestines. Slow boil for 1 hour.
2. Add peeled groundnuts, peppercorns and slow boil another 45 minutes until groundnuts are soft.
3. Add pork, onion, dried floating bladder, 1 tablespoonful light soya sauce, pinch of monosodium glutamate/seasoning and salt to taste. Add water if there is insufficient soup.
4. When pork is cooked, remove dish from heat and serve.

HU PEOW TH'NG
(Dried Floating Bladder Soup)

150 g dried floating bladder, soaked till soft
150 g sea cucumber
225 g chicken meat
4 dried Chinese mushrooms, soaked till soft
1 small carrot
75 g cauliflower
½ tsp light soya sauce
Monosodium glutamate/seasoning (optional)
Salt to taste
Sprig of spring onion, cut in 5 cm lengths
1 big red onion
2 pips garlic
10 white peppercorns
3 tbsp oil

PREPARATION

1. Soak and cut dried floating bladder into pieces.
2. Cut chicken and sea cucumber into pieces.
3. Soak and cut mushrooms into halves.
4. Skin and cut carrot into slices.
5. Cut cauliflower into bite-size pieces.
6. Cut onions into quarters.
7. Mince garlic coarsely.
8. Pound peppercorns lightly till cracked.

METHOD

1. Heat pot, add 3 tablespoonfuls cooking oil. When oil is hot, add minced garlic. Reduce heat, fry till light brown.
2. Add onions and chicken meat, stir for a minute.
3. Add 2½ rice bowls of water, sea cucumber and carrots. Bring to boil.
4. When soup has boiled, add cauliflower, pounded peppercorns, ½ tablespoon light soya sauce, seasoning and salt to taste.
5. Simmer till ingredients are tender and soup thickens. Dish out and add spring onions. Serve.

(OVERLEAF) HU PEOW TH'NG: To experience the richness of this soup, simmer the ingredients over a low flame until they are very tender.

ROASTED PORK AND MUSTARD GREEN SOUP

600 g salted mustard greens (kiam chai)
1 carrot
600 g piece of fleshy roasted pig's leg
225 g roasted pork (siew yoke)
2 pieces tamarind (assam keping)
6 fresh red chillies
10 white peppercorns
2 nutmeg seeds
Monosodium glutamate/seasoning (optional)

PREPARATION

1. Cut salted mustard greens into 5 centimetre lengths.
2. Slice carrot into bite-size pieces.
3. Crack shell of nutmegs and remove seeds and pound open.

METHOD

1. Fill pot with 2½ rice bowls of water, add salted mustard greens, bring to slow boil until vegetables are quite soft. Add extra water if required.
2. When salted mustard greens are soft enough, add 2 rice bowls of water, tamarind pieces, nutmeg seeds, all the roast, peppercorns, carrot and chillies. Simmer until pork is soft enough for personal taste.
3. Add salt to taste and monosodium glutamate/ seasoning if preferred. Serve.

Note:
Periodically taste if the dish is sufficiently sour. Remove tamarind pieces when the soup meets your personal taste.

POH HO TH'NG
(Mint Soup)

4 eggs
1 bunch of mint leaves (daun pudina)
1½ rice bowls of water
2 tbsp cooking oil
Salt
Pepper

PREPARATION

1. Discard mint leaf-stalks. Wash and drain leaves.
2. Beat eggs.

METHOD

1. Put mint leaves into beaten eggs.
2. Heat frying pan. When hot, add oil and pour in the mixed egg and mint leaf mixture.
3. Fry for 1 – 2 minutes. Add 1 ½ rice bowls of water and salt to taste to fried eggs and mint leaves.
4. Bring to boil. Remove from flame and serve.

Note:
Do not fry egg and mint leaves mixture till cooked. The idea is to fry them lightly for under 2 minutes so that egg and mint leaves will stick together.

If you like, sprinkle some fried sliced shallots into the soup before serving. This soup is traditionally eaten to remove wind from the stomach.

PRAWN BALLS IN CABBAGE SOUP

150 g cabbage
300 g prawns
4 pips garlic
1 tbsp light soya sauce
1 level tsp pepper
1 Maggi chicken cube (optional)

PREPARATION

1. Cut cabbage into pieces, wash and drain.
2. Shell prawns, wash, drain and mince. Add 1 tablespoonful light soya sauce and pepper. Mix well. Make prawn balls.
3. Mince garlic.

METHOD

1. Heat pot with 2½ rice bowls of water until it boils. Add cabbage.
2. When cabbage is almost cooked, put prawn balls into the stock. Slow boil until prawns are cooked.
3. Add a little Maggi chicken flavour and salt to taste. Remove from heat.
4. Fry garlic in 3 tablespoonfuls oil till light brown, dish out and put into the soup. Serve.

SPARE RIBS IN PRESERVED SOYA BEAN SOUP

600 g fleshly pork spare ribs
2 medium-sized Chinese radish (lobak putih)
1 tbsp preserved soya bean paste (taucheong)
6 shallots
3 pips garlic
4 slices ginger
6 tbsp cooking oil
Monosodium glutamate/seasoning (optional)

PREPARATION

1. Chop and clean the spare ribs.
2. Skin the radish and cut into triangular shaped pieces.
3. Pound onions and garlic finely.

METHOD

1. Heat pot, add oil. When the oil is hot, add pounded ingredients and ginger slices. Stir until soft. Add preserved soya bean paste and fry until fragrant.
2. Add spare ribs, stir well for 1 minute, add water to cover spare ribs. Slow boil for 10 minutes than add radish.
3. Add a little extra water to cover ingredients and monosodium glutamate/seasoning to taste.
4. Slow boil until spare ribs and radish are soft. Remove from heat and serve.

MEE SUAR SOUP
(Fine Vermicelli Soup)

2 bundles of fine rice vermicelli
40 g dried prawns or 80 g fresh prawns
1 egg
2 pips garlic, minced
3 tbsp cooking oil
Salt
Monosodium glutamate/Maggie chicken cube to taste
  (optional)

PREPARATION

1. Soak the dried prawns for a few minutes, wash and drain. If using fresh prawns, shell, wash and drain.

METHOD

1. Heat pot, add cooking oil, When oil is hot, add minced garlic, stir till soft.
2. Add dried prawns (or fresh prawns), stir for 1 minute then add 2¼ rice bowls of water.
3. Bring to boil, add fine rice vermicelli, a little salt and seasoning to taste.
4. Crack in egg and stir to mix well.
5. Lower heat, simmer awhile till the vermicelli becomes soft. Serve.

BAYAM TH'NG
(Spinach Soup)

300 g young spinach (bayam)
40 g dried prawns
2 shallots
2 rice bowls water
4 tbsp oil
Pepper
Salt

PREPARATION

1. Wash and drain spinach.
2. Wash and drain dried prawns.
3. Slice shallots.

METHOD

1. Fry shallots in oil until transparent.
2. Add dried prawns, stir for a minute, then add water. Bring to boil.
3. Add spinach and salt and pepper to taste. Simmer until limp but do not over cook. Serve.

Kuihs & Desserts

Mouthwatering sweets and desserts are synonymous
with nyonya cuisine. Teatime usually meant a
choice of rich, delectable treats in the form of
glutinous rice based concoctions combined with
coconut milk, palm sugar and screwpine leaf juice.
There were always sumptious delights made from
simple staples such as tapioca, bananas, yam,
green peas or agar-agar.
During festive occasions and weddings a
variety of kuihs were usually offered, each more
irresistable then the next. No wonder there could
never be enough of these creamy, fragrant and
delicate tempters.

PULUT PANGGANG

450 g glutinous rice
2 stalks lemon grass (serai), cut into 5 cm lengths
1 thumb-sized fresh young turmeric (kunyit)
3 fresh red chillies, sliced
5 shallots, sliced
300 g prawns
1 coconut, grated
8 tbsp water
Banana leaves
4 – 5 tbsp oil

PREPARATION

1. Soak glutinous rice in water for 3 – 4 hours. Wash and drain. Set aside.
2. Pound lemon grass, turmeric and chillies finely. Add shallots to the pounded ingredients and pound again till fine.
3. Shell prawns, clean and drain. Mince.
4. Add ¾ rice bowl of water to ½ grated coconut and squeeze for coconut milk. Add a little salt, stir well till it dissolves.
5. Soak banana leaves in boiling water till soft. Remove, clean and cut into 20 pieces of 15 cm x 15 cm.

METHOD

1. Steam glutinous rice for 25 minutes, add coconut milk, mix well. Steam again for another 25 minutes till the rice is cooked. Remove, set aside.
2. Heat a pan, add oil. Then add ½ grated coconut, pounded ingredients, minced prawns and salt to taste. Stir.
3. Reduce heat. Add 8 tablespoonfuls of water and continue stirring until ingredients are about to dry up. Remove and set aside.
4. Place some of the steamed glutinous rice on a banana leaf, add fried ingredients. Cover the filling with more rice.
5. Fold the banana leaf over and roll into a sausage shape. Secure ends with staples or preferably coconut leaf ribs.
6. Toast over charcoal fire, turning it often to ensure even toasting.
7. When banana leaves turn brown and are slightly burnt, remove. Serve.

Note:
Alternately, you could heat 2 tablespoonfuls oil in a kuali on very low flame. Fry pulut panggang in this. Cover for a few minutes. Turn regularly until brown and cooked.

REMPAH UDANG

450 g glutinous rice
225 g shelled prawns, minced
½ coconut, grated
150 g grated coconut, fried until brown
2 tbsp coriander (ketumbar)
3 pieces old ginger
17 white peppercorns
5 shallots
4 pips garlic
2 tbsp sugar
1 tbsp light soya sauce
1 tsp dark soya sauce
6 tbsp cooking oil
Salt
Banana leaves

PREPARATION

1. Grind coriander, pepper seeds and galangal finely. Do the same for shallots and garlic.
2. Soak glutinous rice in water for 3 hours. Clean, drain and steam for 25 minutes.
3. Add 1 rice bowl of water to grated coconut and squeeze for milk. Add a little salt to the milk, stir until it dissolves. Pour coconut milk into steamed glutinous rice and mix well.
4. Steam rice again for another 25 minutes until cooked. Remove and set aside.
5. Pound the fried grated coconut finely.
6. Heat pan, add oil. Add pounded shallots and the ground ingredients. Stir until fragrant. Add minced prawns, light soya sauce, sugar and salt to taste.
7. Soak banana leaves in boiling water until soft. Remove, clean and cut into 25 pieces of 15 centimetre squares.

METHOD

1. Place some steamed glutinous rice on a banana leaf, add the fried ingredients and cover the ingredients with more steamed rice.
2. Fold the banana leaf over and roll into a sausage shape. Secure ends with coconut leaf ribs or toothpicks.
3. Grease pan with oil. Grill rempah udang in a pan turning often, until the leaf is brown and slightly burnt. Remove and serve.

Note:
A charcoal pit is even better for grilling the rempah udang.

KUIH KOCI

600 g glutinous rice, soaked in water for 5 hours
1 tbsp sugar
1 tbsp coconut milk
Some banana leaves

FILLING
¼ young coconut, grated
4 tbsp sugar
2 tbsp brown sugar
1 rice bowl of water
3 screwpine leaves (daun pandan)
3 tbsp tapioca flour

PREPARATION

1. Wash glutinous rice well, add clean water and grind with electric blender till fine. Pour into container. Put the ground glutinous rice into a flour sack and hang to dry. Do this in the evening and by next morning the ground rice will be of a doughy consistency.
2. Soak banana leaves in boiling water till soft, remove and drain.

METHOD

1. Pour the glutinous rice dough into a plate, add one tablespoonful sugar and one tablespoonful coconut milk. Knead till smooth.
2. Heat pan, add one rice bowl of water and brown sugar. Stir till sugar dissolves. Dish out and sieve. Pour the liquid back into the pan, add grated young coconut, screwpine leaves and white sugar. Stir until it starts to thicken. Remove and set aside.
3. Knead the dough into a roll, divide into required portions. Roll dough portions into a ball then roll till flat (if the dough is sticky, add a little tapioca flour), scoop on filling and seal.
4. Rub steaming tray with oil, put kuih koci into the tray and steam until cooked. Remove.
5. Cut banana leaves and shape into cones. Fill with the steamed kuih koci.
6. Wrap up and steam again for 2 – 3 minutes. Remove, cool and serve.

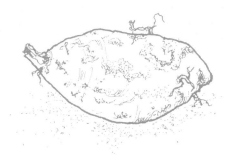

BUBUR CHA CHA

Yet another irresistible tea time temptation — pengat or bubur cha cha: slices of yam, white beans and bananas in a gravy of rich coconut milk and palm sugar.

1 small red sweet potato
1 small yellow sweet potato
150 g yam
2 pisang raja
75 g white beans
100 g tapioca flour
¾ coconut, grated
225 g sugar
½ tsp salt
3 – 4 screwpine leaves (daun pandan), washed, torn down the middle and knotted
Artificial food colouring

PREPARATION

1. Skin sweet potatoes, wash, drain and cut into cubes.
2. Cut yam into 2 centimetre cubes.
3. Skin pisang raja and cut diagonally into pieces 2 centimetres thick.
4. Soak white beans in water for 3 hours. Clean and boil in sufficient water until soft but make sure beans do not split.
5. Add some water to the tapioca flour and knead into a dough; add a little red colouring, knead again and roll into a thin strip. Cut into strips of 2.5 centimetres.
6. Add 1 rice bowl of water to the grated coconut and squeeze for first milk. Add another 3 rice bowls of water and squeeze for second milk.

METHOD

1. Boil the tapioca pieces in water. When cooked, take out and dip into cold water. Remove and set aside.
2. Fill pot with second coconut milk and yam cubes. Bring to a boil till it is half cooked.
3. Add sweet potato cubes, screwpine leaves and slow boil until potato and yam cubes are cooked.
4. Add bananas, cooked white beans, cooked tapioca pieces, sugar and salt to taste.
5. If the gravy is not rich enough, add additional water to the grated coconut and squeeze for third milk. Add required amount.
6. Taste for sweetness, adjust accordingly. Bring to boil, add first coconut milk until it is rich enough.
7. Boil again for 1 to 2 minutes. Remove from heat. Serve with coloured tapioca flour strips.

KUIH EE

500 g glutinous rice flour dough
375 g sugar
2 cm ginger, pounded open
4 screwpine leaves (daun pandan)
Red and yellow colouring

PREPARATION

1. Break off two 75 g pieces dough. Add a little yellow colouring to each and knead until they become just yellow.
2. Break off another two 75 g pieces of dough. Add a little red colouring to each and knead until they become just red.
3. Break off some of the white dough and roll into a ball the size of a marble. Repeat till all the white dough is finished.
4. Do the same for the red and yellow dough but halve the size of the dough balls.
5. Wash screwpine leaves. Tear into two down the middle and knot.

METHOD

1. Half fill pot with water, and bring to boil. Add in the white dough balls a few at a time taking care that they do not cluster and stick together. When they float to the top, they are cooked. Dish out and put into another pot half filled with cold water.
2. Repeat for the red and yellow dough balls.
3. Fill a small pot with 3 rice bowls of water and bring to boil. Add screwpine leaves, ginger and sugar until sufficiently sweet for personal taste. Boil on low flame for 8 minutes until all the sugar is dissolved. Set aside to cool.
4. Dish out the kuih ee from the cold water, drain off the water and add to the sweet soup. Serve in individual bowls.

Note:
Kuih ee dough is made from finely ground glutinous rice flour.

KUIH EE: Red, white and round, kuih ee is symbolic of complete happiness and purity in nyonya tradition. This sweet is served at weddings and the Winter Festival.

SERIKAYA
(Rich Egg and Coconut Jam)

This classic home-made jam is unbeatable in taste as a spread on breads, biscuits or glutinous rice cakes.

1 big coconut, grated
3 A-sized eggs
300 g sugar
2 – 3 screwpine leaves (daun pandan)
2 tbsp sugar

PREPARATION

1. Squeeze a thick concentrated coconut cream from grated coconut in a piece of muslin. Add no water to coconut. Set aside.
2. Beat eggs and add 300 g sugar into it. Beat mixture with a wooden spoon till sugar dissolves. Do not beat too hard.
3. Wash and tear screwpine leaves into two down the middle and knot up.

METHOD

1. Bring half a large pot of water to the boil. Lower heat and keep water below boiling point.
2. Select a container that will fit into the pot. Fill container with beaten sugar and egg, coconut milk and screwpine leaves. Mix well.
3. Lower container into the large pot to steam. Stir mixture with wooden spoon continuously for about 15 to 20 minutes to prevent any curdling. Stir till a custard-like consistency is obtained.
4. Meanwhile, heat two tablespoonfuls sugar in a ladle until it melts and turns brown. Add quickly into coconut milk and egg mixture and stir well.
5. Remove container from pot and wrap a piece of cloth firmly round the top. This is to prevent steam from entering the jam.
6. Put container back into steaming pot, cover lid and steam on medium heat for 2 hours.
7. To prevent curdling and to ensure that the coconut jam has a smooth consistency, stir it once or twice in between after removing the cloth from the container. Rewrap the cloth each time after stirring.
8. The water level in the pot must be maintained throughout the process of steaming.
9. Turn heat off after two hours. Allow jam to cool. Store in bottles or jars. Serve.

Note:
More eggs may be added for a variation of texture and flavour. Increase sugar only accordingly.

SAGO PUDDING

125 g fine sago
1 coconut, grated
1 round piece of palm sugar (gula Melaka)
Salt to taste
2 – 3 screwpine leaves (daun pandan)
Colouring (optional)

PREPARATION

1. Squeeze grated coconut for milk after adding a cup of water.
2. Wash screwpine leaves, tear it down the middle and knot up.

METHOD

1. Boil the palm sugar and screwpine leaves in a cup of water. Keep boiling until palm sugar is completely dissolved.
2. Taste for sweetness. Add a little sugar if you want a sweeter syrup. Remove to cool and chill in the fridge.
3. Do the same for coconut milk after adding a pinch of salt.
4. Boil water in a separate pot, and add a pinch of salt. When water has boiled, add sago. When grains become transparent, the sago is cooked.
5. Drain off excess water through sieve but don't rinse the sago. Transfer sago into a container or a bowl.
6. Add colouring to sago (optional). Chill.
7. To serve, spoon portions of sago into dish and smother with coconut milk and syrup.

GORENG PISANG
(Banana Fritters)

6 pisang raja
150 g flour
3 tbsp rice flour
1 level tsp baking powder
1 level tsp salt

PREPARATION

1. Remove skin of bananas, clean and slice into half, lengthwise.

METHOD

1. Sieve flour and rice flour into a bowl. Add baking powder and salt. Stir until ingredients are well mixed.

2. Add water little by little till you get a smooth batter that is not too watery or thick. If too watery, the batter will not coat banana pieces well, if too thick, you will end up with a hard crust.
3. Heat frying pan, add enough oil for deep frying. The oil has to be hot before you fry the bananas or the batter will drip off.
4. Coat the banana in the batter and slip it down the edge of the frying pan into the oil. Keep turning till cooked. Regulate heat so that banana does not burn.
5. Remove, drain on kitchen paper napkins. Serve.

Note:
If using sweet potato or yam instead, clean, dry and cut into 1.2 centimetre slices. Dip into same batter and deep fry.

SERIKAYA: It is a good nyonya cook who can proudly serve up this perfect coconut jam.

SAGO PUDDING: Sprinkle a little grated gula Melaka on the pudding for an interesting presentation.

TAPIOCA IN SWEET GRAVY

600 g tapioca
150 g brown sugar
150 g white sugar
½ coconut, grated
4 screwpine leaves (daun pandan)

PREPARATION

1. Skin tapioca, remove core, clean and cut into 6 centimetre lengths.
2. Add 1 rice bowl of water to grated coconut and squeeze for first milk. Set aside. Add another 1½ rice bowls of water to squeeze for second milk. Dissolve the above brown sugar into second milk and sieve.

METHOD

1. Put tapioca into a pot. Add water till tapioca is covered.
2. Add 2 screwpine leaves. Slow boil till tapioca is soft. Remove and drain.

GRAVY

1. Into a heated pan add second coconut milk, brown sugar mixture, white sugar and 2 screwpine leaves. Slow boil until sugar dissolves.
2. Then add tapioca, first coconut milk and salt to taste. Stir for a few seconds and remove.

Note:
If gravy is not sweet enough, add additional sugar.

KUIH TAYAP

BATTER
140g plain flour
⅔ rice bowl milk
1 egg
¼ tsp salt
8 screwpine leaves (daun pandan)

FILLING
½ young coconut, grated
150 g brown sugar
1¼ rice bowls water

PREPARATION

1. Pound 6 screwpine leaves till fine, add 1 tablespoonful water and squeeze out the green juice. Set aside.
2. Sieve flour.

METHOD

1. Beat 1 egg into the milk, stir in the flour and slowly add water while stirring until the dough becomes smooth and very soft. Add screwpine juice until the dough is sufficiently green. Add ¼ to ½ teaspoon salt and stir well. Set aside.
2. Heat pan at medium fire, add water and brown sugar. Stir till sugar dissolves. Dish out, cool and sieve to remove unwanted particles.
3. Heat pan again, add sugar mixture, grated coconut and 2 screwpine leaves. Fry until mixture starts to thicken. Remove heat and dish out.
4. Heat pan at medium fire till hot. Rub on oil margarine. Pour in 3 tablespoonfuls batter (beat the batter first). Swivel the pan by holding the two ears of the pan with cloth until the batter spreads into a round thin piece. Turn crepe over when the bottom side is cooked. Keep turning until both sides are slightly brown. Repeat the method till all the batter is finished.
5. Take a crepe and scoop some filling onto it. Fold opposite sides inwards and roll to make an elongated pillow. Repeat till crepe is used up. Serve.

KUIH BENGKA UBI KAYU

1 kg tapioca (ubi kayu)
1 coconut, grated
300 g sugar
2 tbsp tapioca flour
Banana leaves
6 screwpine leaves (daun pandan)

PREPARATION

1. Skin tapioca and clean. Grate and set aside.
2. Add 1½ rice bowls of water to coconut and squeeze for milk.
3. Soak banana leaves in boiling water till soft. Remove and cut into pieces for lining baking tray.

METHOD

1. Put grated tapioca into a container or big bowl. Add coconut milk, sugar, tapioca flour. Stir to mix well.
2. Place a layer of banana leaves into a baking tray that is at least 12.5 centimetres in depth. Put on a second layer of leaves and also line sides of tray. On top of this second layer place screwpine leaves.
3. Put tapioca mixture on top.
4. Bake in an oven at 180°C until brown. Remove, let it cool before serving.

BEE KOH

600 g glutinous rice
1 big coconut, grated
300 g brown sugar
115 g white sugar
1 tsp tapioca flour
8 screwpine leaves (daun pandan)
Banana leaf

PREPARATION

1. Soak glutinous rice in water for 6 hours, wash and drain. Place 4 screwpine leaves into a steaming tray, spread the rice on top and steam until it is cooked. Set aside.
2. Add 2 rice bowls of water to grated coconut to squeeze for first milk.
3. Heat 2½ rice bowls of coconut milk in a kuali, add brown sugar, stirring constantly until the brown sugar dissolves. Remove from heat, let mixture cool, sieve.
4. Mix 1 teaspoonful tapioca flour in 2 tablespoonfuls coconut milk till a smooth consistency is obtained.
5. Put a layer of banana leaf into a steaming tray.

METHOD

1. Heat a kuali, pour in the sieved solution of coconut milk and brown sugar, add white sugar, slow boil until sugar is dissolved.
2. Add cooked glutinous rice, stir continously until it starts to thicken and add the dissolved tapioca flour and stir quickly 2 to 3 times.
3. Dish out into the tray. With the back of a tablespoon, smoothen the surface by applying slight pressure. Leave to cool until it hardens. Slice and serve.

APUM MANIS

1 cup of high grade rice
½ coconut, grated
¾ level tsp baking powder
¼ tsp salt
1 tbsp sugar
Cooking oil

PREPARATION

1. Soak rice in water overnight, discard water, wash rice.
2. Put ½ the rice into electric blender, add a little water and grind finely (do not add too much water because coconut milk is to be added later; the batter has to be as thick as possible).
3. Pour the batter into a mixing bowl or container. Add baking powder, sugar and salt.
4. Add coconut milk slowly stirring well until batter is just slightly watery. Leave aside for 3 hours.
5. Whip batter well just before cooking.

METHOD

1. Heat kuali or small pan until hot (do not overheat). Use a clean cloth to rub pan with cooking oil.
2. Stir the batter well. Scoop 3 tablespoonfuls into the pan. Quickly lift the 2 ears of the pan and swivel to make the batter spread well and evenly (about 14 cm in diameter).
3. Put down the pan and let the batter set and cook. Scrape the side with a metal spatula and dish out. Serve.

LEPAT PISANG

11 ripe pisang awak
180 g flour
90 g sugar
½ coconut, grated
½ tsp salt
Banana leaves

PREPARATION

1. Skin bananas, clean, and mash bananas till fine.
2. Add 1 rice bowl of water to grated coconut and squeeze for milk.
3. Soak banana leaves in boiling water till soft. Remove, clean and dry with cloth. Cut into 12.5 cm x 22.5 cm pieces.

METHOD

1. Put flour, mashed bananas, sugar, ½ teaspoon salt into mixing bowl and slowly add some coconut milk. Stir till it becomes a soft dough. Beat well, add remainder of the coconut milk into dough. It should not be too watery or thick.
2. Roll a banana leaf into a cylindrical shape. Fold one end up. Fill the leaf packet with dough from the open end. Seal end and fasten with staple or toothpick.
3. Put on a steaming tray and steam for 10 to 15 minutes. Remove, cool and serve.

KUIH KASUI

300 g palm sugar (gula Melaka)
150 g brown sugar
120 g sugar   (A)
2½ rice bowls water
2 screwpine leaves (daun pandan)

600 g flour
¼ tsp slaked lime (kapor)
½ tsp salt
2½ rice bowls water
250 g grated coconut, white
pinch of fine salt

PREPARATION

1. Sieve flour into a large bowl.
2. Dissolve ¼ tsp slaked lime and ½ tsp salt in 2½ rice bowls water.
3. Mix the grated coconut with a pinch of fine salt.

METHOD

1. Put ingredients (A) and 2½ rice bowls water into a sauce pan and heat till sugar dissolves. Stir occasionally. Strain syrup.
2. Add slaked lime and salt solution to flour gradually. Mix till consistency is smooth.
3. Add luke warm syrup a little at a time to batter. Stir well, strain mixture.
4. Pour mixture into a deep tray and steam for ½ hour.
5. When cooked, cool and cut into diamond-shaped pieces. Roll in grated coconut. Serve.

Note:

Small individual moulds can also be used for steaming the kuih; heat the empty moulds in steamer for 2 – 3 minutes before using.

PULUT HITAM (BEE KO MOI)

(Black Glutinous Rice Porridge)

150 g black glutinous rice
150 g glutinous rice
1 coconut, grated
Sugar
Salt
4 screwpine leaves

PREPARATION

1. Wash black glutinous rice and glutinous rice. Put into a pot, and add 2 rice bowls of water.
2. Add 1 rice bowl of water to grated coconut and squeeze for first milk, add a pinch of salt, stir until it dissolves.
3. Wash screwpine leaves and knot after tearing in two down the middle.

METHOD

1. Boil glutinous rice mixture. Add screwpine leaves and bring to slow boil until it starts to thicken. Stir often to prevent sticking to the pot.
2. Check to see if the mixture is cooked, if it is not, add some water and continue boiling. Remember to keep stirring.
3. When the porridge is fully cooked and starts to thicken, add water and sugar until it is sweet enough. Bring to boil until it starts to thicken again. Remove from heat. It should not be watery nor too thick.

Serving:

Scoop porridge into a bowl. Add 1 to 2 tablespoonfuls coconut milk and serve.

GANDUM

150 g bulgur wheat (gandum)
150 g brown sugar
150 g white sugar
1 medium-sized coconut, grated
¼ tsp salt
4 screwpine leaves (daun pandan)

PREPARATION

1. Clean and wash bulgur wheat after soaking in water for 2 hours.
2. Add 1 rice bowl of water to grated coconut, squeeze for first milk.

(FACING PAGE) *PULUT HITAM & GANDUM: Two popular nyonya porridges served with coconut milk shown here bottled hawker style.*

3. Add 3 rice bowls of water to the same coconut and squeeze for second milk.
4. Dissolve brown sugar in the second coconut milk. Sieve.

METHOD

1. Pour bulgur wheat into a pot with 3 rice bowls of water. Boil over medium heat.
2. After boiling for 15 minutes, stir the bulgur wheat often till it starts to thicken. Add water until the consistency is fluid. Slow boil until it turns into a thick porridge.
3. Wash the screwpine leaves. Tear it down the middle and knot them up. Put into pot, add second coconut milk until porridge is watery again. Keep stirring often to prevent bulgur wheat from sticking to pot.
4. Add white sugar and ½ teaspoon salt and bring to boil again. Keep stirring often.
5. Add first coconut milk, boil for another few minutes. If porridge is too thick, add more coconut milk until the consistency is to your liking.
6. Lower heat, boil again and serve.

STEAMED PULUT AND WHITE BEANS

100 g white beans
450 g glutinous rice
3 screwpine leaves (daun pandan)
1 coconut, grated
5 big pisang raja, or 6 – 7 small ones
Banana leaves

PREPARATION

1. Soak white beans in water for 3 hours. Wash, drain. Put into a pot, cover beans with water and boil until soft. Make sure beans do not split. Set aside.
2. Soak glutinous rice in water for 3 hours. Wash and drain.
3. Cut screwpine leaves into 5 centimetre strips. Put this into the clean glutinous rice and steam for 25 minutes. Set aside.
4. Add ¾ rice bowl of water to grated coconut and squeeze for first milk. Add a little salt, stir well till it dissolves. Set aside.
5. Remove skin of pisang raja. Slice lengthwise and cut each slice into two.
6. Soak banana leaves in boiling water until soft. Remove and clean. Cut into 20 pieces of 15 centimetre squares.

METHOD

1. Pour coconut milk into the steamed glutinous rice and add the cooked white beans. Mix well.
2. Remove screwpine leaves. Scoop some of the mixture on the banana leaves, add a piece of banana. Cover banana with a little more of the mixture.
3. Wrap into a sausage roll shape and tuck in the two ends neatly.
4. Tie the ends with a string or hemp.
5. Steam for about 35 minutes. Serve.

ABOK ABOK SAGO

Abok Abok Sago is a concoction of sago, coconut milk and palm sugar steamed in banana leaves. An easy dessert to make, it is nonetheless always a winner.

225 g sago
10 screwpine leaves (daun pandan)
300 g young coconut, grated
150 g brown sugar
115 g white sugar
2 – 3 banana leaves, cut into 10 – 12 cm squares
Pinch of salt

PREPARATION

1. Wash sago and drain in a sieve. Put sago into a metal container or bowl. Fill with water until water level is about 2.5 centimetres above sago.
2. Wash and clean screwpine leaves. Cut into pieces and pound finely. Add water and squeeze for 1 rice bowl of screwpine juice. Set aside 4 tablespoonfuls of grated coconut and add daun pandan juice to the remainder.
3. Add the 4 tablespoonfuls of the grated coconut to the sago and stir in white and brown sugar.
4. Mix the grated coconut with screwpine juice and the sago mixture. Set aside.

METHOD

1. Fold banana leaves into conical shapes. Fill with sago and coconut mixture. Press to make sago compact.
2. When the cone has been filled, bend the edges down to cover the top and secure with a coconut leaf rib.
3. Steam for ½ to ¾ hours. Test one cone to see whether sago mixture has been sufficiently cooked. Remove from heat. Serve.

Note:
Alternately, line a steaming tray with a layer or two of banana leaves and pour sago mixture into tray. Flatten and steam. To serve, cut into pieces with a wet knife.

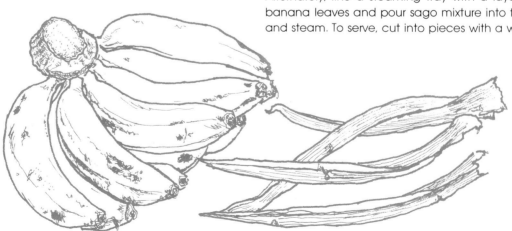

CHOPADAK UBI KAYU

600 g tapioca (ubi kayu)
Approximately ½ rice bowl of tapioca flour
225 g prawns, mince after leaving 20 with shells intact
150 g grated young coconut
1 stalk lemon grass (serai), cut into 5 cm slices
3 fresh red chillies
Thumb-sized piece fresh young turmeric (kunyit)
2 shallots
2 pips garlic
2 – 3 tbsp oil
Pinch of salt

PREPARATION

1. Skin tapioca. Cut into 6 centimetre lengths. Wash, drain and boil till soft. Remove and mash. Add salt, tapioca flour and knead into a soft dough.
2. Shell prawns. Wash, drain and mince coarsely.
3. Wash, drain and set aside 20 whole prawns.
4. Pound lemon grass, chillies and turmeric finely. Slice onion and add to the above pounded ingredients
* and pound again till fine.

METHOD

1. Heat a pan. Add young grated coconut, pounded ingredients, 8 tablespoonfuls of water, minced prawns and a little salt. Stir well until ingredients are about to dry up. Remove and set aside.
2. Take a small lump of tapioca dough and roll into a ball then roll till flat. Add the fried mixture as filling and fold the dough to seal the edges.
3. Place an unshelled prawn on top, pressing it in slightly with your finger. Repeat with the remaining dough.
4. Heat a pan. Add enough oil for deep frying. When oil is hot, fry till brown. Serve.

ONDEH ONDEH

280 g glutinous rice flour
10 screwpine leaves
1 block palm sugar (gula Melaka)
200 g grated coconut, white
Salt

PREPARATION

1. Chop screwpine leaves finely and pound till fine. Add 1 tablespoonful hot water and squeeze in muslin cloth to extract juice. Set aside.
2. Grate palm sugar.
3. Preheat ½ a deep saucepan water.

METHOD

1. Sieve glutinous rice flour with a pinch of salt. Add water and screwpine juice a little at a time. Combine and knead to a smooth dough. Cover dough with a damp cloth to prevent drying.
2. Take a small lump of dough. Flatten and put some grated palm sugar in the middle. Seal palm sugar with dough and roll into a ball. Repeat till all the dough is used up.
3. Bring water to a boil. Drop dough balls in rapidly boiling water. When dough balls rise to the surface, remove. Drain and roll in grated coconut. Serve.

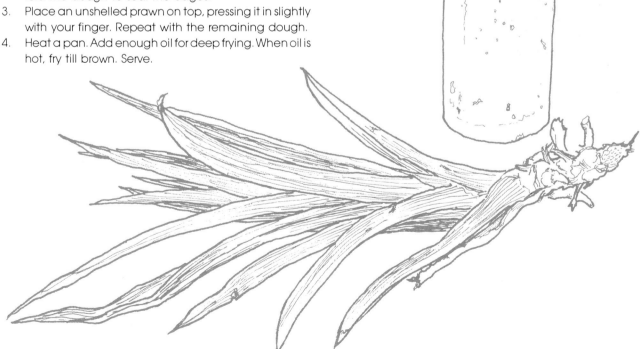

BEE THYE BUCK

Bee thye buck are short muti-coloured sago strips. They are available in their dried form from Indonesian provision shops. It was a nyonya favourite, appearing in the old days at wedding lunches in a syrup.

300 g bee thye buck
3 screwpine leaves (daun pandan)
3 rice bowls water
Sugar to taste

PREPARATION

1. Wash dried sago strips and soak in cold water for 20 minutes. Drain and set aside.
2. Wash screwpine leaves. Drain and slit each leaf down the middle. Knot.

METHOD

1. Fill a pot with 3 rice bowls of water. Add screwpine leaves and bring to the boil. Reduce heat and add sugar to taste. Simmer till sugar dissolves.
2. When sugar is dissolved, add sago strips and slow boil till strips expand leaving a little uncooked strip in the core. Remove strips from syrup and drain.
3. Cool syrup in refrigerator and add in sago strips.

KUIH KODOK

11 fairly big pisang awak (choose bananas that are quite ripe so the kuih will taste sweet)
180 g flour
¼ tsp salt
1 tsp baking powder
Oil for deep frying

PREPARATION

1. Skin bananas, wash and drain. Mash till fine.
2. Add flour (no water is required), ¼ teaspoon salt and baking powder.
3. Knead well until it becomes a smooth soft dough.

METHOD

1. Heat oil for deep frying.
2. Reduce heat and fry dollops of dough. Turn often until brown. Dish out, drain and serve.

BEE THYE BUCK: Pretty to look at, delightful to taste.

AGAR AGAR SANTAN

75 g agar agar, divide into three equal parts
20 screwpine leaves (daun pandan)
½ coconut, grated
300 g sugar
Salt to taste

PREPARATION

1. Wash, drain screwpine leaves and cut into small pieces. Pound finely and squeeze for juice. Add screwpine juice to 6 rice bowls of water until it has a nice green colouring.
2. Pour 1½ rice bowls of the screwpine water into the grated coconut and squeeze for first milk. Set aside.

METHOD

1. Pour remaining screwpine water into a kettle or pot. Add 2 parts of the agar agar and sugar. Bring to boil at medium heat until the agar agar is completely dissolved. Test if mixture is sweet enough. Adjust if necessary.
2. Sieve mixture. Pour into a jelly mould till it is half full.
3. Cool and put in fridge to set.
4. When the agar agar has set, fill a small pot with the first coconut milk, add remaining 1 part of the agar agar and bring to boil at medium heat until it is completely dissolved.
5. Remove quickly and pour mixture through a metal sieve over first layer.
6. Cool and put, once again, in fridge to set.
7. Serve cut into pieces.

Note:

Do not overboil the coconut milk and agar agar mixture or it will turn very oily. Artificial food colouring can be substituted for natural screwpine juice colouring.

AGAR AGAR SANTAN: A quick and easy dessert which is served here in the shape of the British Lion.

INDEX

Abok Abok Sago 136
Agar Agar 11
   Agar Agar Santan 139
Apum Manis 133
Abalone
   Pau Hu Th'ng 116
Acar
   Acar Awak (1) 36
   Acar Awak (2) 36
   Acar Betik 37
   Acar Kunyit Ikan 40
   Acar Limau 35
   Acar Nanas 34
   Mango Acar 39, 40
   Purut Ikan 38
   Salt Fish Acar 37
Anchovy, Dried
   Fried Anchovies with Groundnuts 87
   Green Chillie Sambal 55
Anchovy, Fresh
   Fresh Anchovy Fry Omelette 87
   Sambal Ikan Bilis 57
Assam Fish 82
Ayam Kuning (Kunyit) 67
Ayam Limau Purut 68
Ayam Panggang Satay 66

Bah Ywe Pho in Taucheong 74
Banana
   Goreng Pisang 131
   Kuih Kodok 138
   Lepat Pisang 133
Banana Bud
   Jantung Pisang Gulai Lemak 48
   Jantung Pisang Kerabu 26
Bayam Masak Lemak 94
Bayam Th'ng 123
Beansprouts
   Fried Salt Fish with Taugeh 94
   Heh Kian Taugeh 25
   Kerabu Taugeh 101
Bee Koh 133
Bee Thye Buck 138
Beef Fried with Cauliflower 95
Betik Masak Titek 25
Birthday Mee 113
Bittergourd Gulai 44
Bosomboh 18

Brinjal
   Fried Brinjals in Soya Bean Paste 92
   Gulai Lemak Brinjals or Long Beans 45, 46
   Sambal Belacan Brinjals 60
Bubur Cha Cha 127
Bulgur Wheat
   Gandum 134, 135

Cabbage
   Kobis Masak Lemak (1) 100
   Kobis Masak Lemak (2) 100
   Prawn Balls in Cabbage Soup 122
Candlenuts 11
Cauliflower
   Beef Fried with Cauliflower 95
Chap Chai Lemak 92
Chicken
   Ayam Kuning (Kunyit) 67
   Ayam Limau Purut 68
   Ayam Panggang Satay 66
   Chicken Innards Fried with Cucumber 67
   Enche Kebin 69
   Fried Chicken Nyonya Style 67
   Gulai Ayam 52
   Gulai Nasi Kunyit 43
   Hu Peow Th'ng 119, 120
   Hot Spice Chicken 66
   Nyonya Chicken Porridge 105
   Sar Keong Chicken 66
Chicken Innards Fried with Cucumber 67
Chinchalok with Chillies 61
Chinese Celery
   Sotong Fried Kin Chai 95
Chopadak Ubi Kayu 137
Cockle
   Gulai Salt Fish Pineapple 48
   Kerang Kucai Goreng 92, 93
   Sambal Tumis Kerang 56
Coconut Milk 11, 139
Cooking Terms 14
Coriander Leaves 11
Crab
   Crab Gulai 50
   Sweet Sour Crab 80, 81
Curries
  (See Gulai)
Curry Leaves 11

Cuttlefish
    Jiu Hu Char with Sengkuang   96
    Sotong Fried Kin Chai   95

Daun Kesom
    (See Polygonum)
Daun Limau Purut   11, 68
Daun Pandan
    (See Screwpine Leaves)
Daun Pudina
    (See Mint)
Daun Ubi Keledek Masak Lemak   95
Desserts
    (See also Kuihs)
    Agar Agar Santan   139
    Bee Thye Buck   138
    Bubur Cha Cha   127
    Gandum   134, 135
    Goreng Pisang   131
    Kuih Ee   128, 129
    Lepat Pisang   133
    Pulut Hitam   134, 135
    Sago Pudding   131
    Serikaya   129, 130
    Tapioca in Sweet Gravy   132
Dried Prawns
    Egg and Cucumber Kerabu   101
    Fried Kangkong or Long Beans with Dried Prawns   97
    Jantung Pisang Kerabu   26
    Sambal Heh Bee   57
Duck
    Kiam Chai Arp   117
    Sar Keong Duck   66

Egg and Cucumber Kerabu   101
Eggs, Fresh
    Egg and Cucumber Kerabu   101
    Fresh Anchovy Fry Omelette   87
    Poh Ho Th'ng   122
    Serikaya   129, 130
Eggs, Salted
    Salted Chicken Eggs   28
    Salted Duck Eggs   28
    Pork Steamed with Salted Egg   75
Enche Kebin   69

Five Spice Powder   11
Fresh Anchovy Fry Omelette   87
Fresh Shrimp Fry   12
Fried Anchovies with Groundnuts   87
Fried And Pounded Grated Coconut   12
Fried Brinjals in Soya Bean Paste   92
Fried Chicken Nyonya Style   67
Fried Ikan Bawal Putih with Taucheong   89
Fried Kangkong or Long Beans with Dried Prawns   97
Fried Kiam Chai with Pork   75

Fried Soya Bean Cake and Long Beans   94
Fried Salt Fish with Taugeh   94
Fried Stuffed Taukua   28
Frying a Rempah   14

Gado Gado   20
Galangal   12
Gandum   134, 135
Gerago
    (See Fresh Shrimp Fry)
Golden Needles   12
Glutinous Rice
    Bee Koh   133
    Kuih Ee   128, 129
    Kuih Kochi   127
    Nasi Kunyit   43, 106
    Nyonya Kiam Tn'eo Chang   21
    Ondeh Ondeh   137
    Pulut Panggang   126
    Rempah Udang   126
    Steamed Pulut and White Beans   136
Glutinous Rice, Black
    Pulut Hitam   134, 135
Grinding   14
Groundnuts
    Fried Anchovies with Groundnuts   87
Goreng Pisang   131
Gulai
    Bittergourd Gulai   44
    Crab Gulai   50
    Gulai Ayam   52
    Gulai Ikan Nyonya Style   49
    Gulai Lemak Brinjals or Long Beans   45, 46
    Gulai Lemak Kepala Ikan Kering   44
    Gulai Lemak Nanas   42
    Gulai Nangka   45, 46
    Gulai Nasi Kunyit   43
    Gulai Salt Fish Pineapple   48
    Gulai Tumis Kepala Ikan   50, 51
    Jantung Pisang Gulai Lemak   48
    Pork Gulai Nyonya Style   49

Heh Kian   25
Heh Kian Taugeh   25
Hong Bak   77
Hot Spice Chicken   66
Hu Peow Pig's Intestine Soup   119
Hu Peow Th'ng   119, 120
Hokkien Mee   108

Ikan Assam Pedas   86
Ikan Cencaru Sumbat   88
Ikan Kuning   86
Ikan Masak Assam Kicap   83
Ikan Panggang   83, 84
Ikan Pari Fried in Kiam Chai   82

Jackfruit
    Gulai Nangka 45, 46
Jantung Pisang 11
    Jantung Pisang Gulai Lemak 48
    Jantung Pisang Kerabu 26
Jiu Hu Char with Ubi Sengkuang 96

Kerabu
    Egg and Cucumber Kerabu 101
    Kerabu Taugeh 101
    Kerabu Meehoon 109
Kerang Kuchai Goreng 92, 93
Kiam Chai Arp 117
Kiam Hu Branda 29
Kobis Masak Lemak (1) 100
Kobis Masak Lemak (2) 100
Krisek
    (See Fried and Pounded Grated Coconut)
Kuihs
    (See also Desserts)
    Abok Abok Sago 136
    Apum Manis 133
    Bee Koh 133
    Chopadak Ubi Kayu 137
    Kuih Bengka Ubi Kayu 132
    Kuih Kasui 134
    Kuih Kochi 127
    Kuih Kodok 138
    Kuih Tayap 132
    Ondeh Ondeh 137
    Pulut Panggang 126
    Rempah Udang 126
    Steamed Pulut and White Beans 136
    Kuih Ee 128, 129

Lady's Fingers
    Sambal Bendi 62
La La Fried in Taucheong 29
Lard
    Bah Ywe Pho in Taucheong 74
Lemon Grass 12
Lepat Pisang 133
Lobak 27
Long Beans
    Fried Kangkong or Long Beans with Dried Prawns 97
    Fried Soya Bean Cake and Long Beans 94
    Gulai Lemak Brinjals or Long Beans 45

Mango
    Mango Acar 39, 40
    Sambal Mango 55
Mee Goreng 112
Mee Rebus 105
Mee Suar Soup 123
Mint
    Poh Hoh Th'ng 122

Mussels
    La La Fried in Taucheong 29

Nasi Kunyit 43, 106
Nasi Lemak 110
Nasi Minyak 104
Nasi Ulam/Nasi Kerabu 111
Noodles
    Birthday Mee 113
    Hokkien Mee 108
    Indian Mee/Kuih Teow Goreng 112
    Kerabu Meehoon 109
    Mee Rebus 105
    Penang Asam Laksa 106, 107
    Siamese Laksa 104
Northern Nyonya Specialties
    Betik Masak Titek 25
    Bosomboh 18, 19
    Fried Stuffed Taukua 28
    Sauce for, 26
    Gado Gado 20
    Heh Kian 25
    Heh Kian Taugeh 25
    Jantung Pisang Gulai Lemak 26
    Jantung Pisang Kerabu 26
    Kiam Hu Branda 29
    La La Fried in Taucheong 29
    Lobak 27
    Nyonya Kiam Tn'ee Chang 21, 22
    Otak Otak 24
    Penang Rojak 20
    Po Piah 30, 31
    Po Piah Chien 31
    Pork and Chestnut Dumplings 21, 22
    Roti Babi 24
    Salted Chicken Eggs 28
    Salted Duck Eggs 28
Nutmeg 12
Nyonya Chap Chai 97, 98
Nyonya Chicken Porridge 105
Nyonya Fried Rice 109
Nyonya Kiam Tn'ee Chang 21, 22
Nyonya Prawn Porridge 108

Ondeh Ondeh 137
Otak Otak 24

Palm Sugar 12, 131, 134, 137
Papaya
    Acar Betik 37
    Betik Masak Titek 25
Pau Hu Th'ng 116
Pee Hu Char 86
Penang Assam Laksa 106, 107
Penang Rojak 20

Petai
    Sambal Udang Petai 63
Pickles
    (See Acar)
Pig's Intestines
    Hu Peow Pig's Intestines Soup 119
Pineapple
    Acar Nanas 34
    Gulai Lemak Nanas 42
    Gulai Salt Fish Pineapple 48
    Sambal Timun Nanas 60
Poh Ho Th'ng 122
Polygonum 12
Po Piah 30, 31
Po Piah Chien 31
Pork
    Fried Kiam Chai with Pork 75
    Hong Bak 77
    Hu Peow Pig's Intestines Soup 119
    Lobak 27
    Pork and Chestnut Dumplings 21, 22
    Pork Gulai Nyonya Style 49
    Pork Leg in Black Vinegar 74
    Pork Patties 75
    Pork Satay 72, 73
    Pork Steamed with Salted Egg 75
    Roasted Pork and Mustard Green Soup 122
    Roti Babi 24
    Spare Ribs in Preserved Soya Bean Soup 123
    Sweet Sour Spare Ribs 76
    Tau Yew Bak 77
Poultry
    (See Chicken)
Pounding 14
Prawns, Fresh
    Egg and Cucumber Kerabu 101
    Fried Stuffed Taukua 28
    Gulai Lemak Nanas 42
    Nyonya Prawn Porridge 108
    Prawn Fritters 25
    Prawn Balls in Cabbage Soup 122
    Pulut Panggang 126
    Rempah Udang 126
    Sambal Goreng Udang 54
    Sambal Goreng Udang Assam 56
    Sambal Udang Petai 63
Prawns, Dried
    (See Dried Prawns)
Prawn Paste 12
    Penang Assam Laksa 106, 107
    Penang Rojak 20
Pulut Hitam 134, 135
Pulut Panggang 126
Purut Ikan 38

Rempah Udang 126

Rice
    Nasi Kunyit 43, 106
    Nasi Lemak 110
    Nasi Minyak 104
    Nasi Ulam/Nasi Kerabu 111
    Nyonya Chicken Porridge 105
    Nyonya Fried Rice 109
    Nyonya Prawn Porridge 108
Rice, Glutinous
    (See Glutinous Rice)
Roasted Pork and Mustard Green Soup 122
Roti Babi 24

Sago Pudding 131
Salted Chicken Eggs 28
    Pork Steamed with Salted Egg 75
Salted Duck Eggs 28
Salt Fish
    Fried Salt Fish with Taugeh 94
    Gulai Salt Fish Pineapple 48
    Kiam Hu Char 83
    Kiam Hu Branda 29
    Pee Hu Char 86
    Salt Dish Acar 37
    Salt Fish Soya Bean Soup 118
Salted Mustard Greens
    Fried Kiam Chai with Pork 75
    Ikan Pari Fried with Kiam Chai 82
    Kiam Chai Arp 117
    Roasted Pork and Mustard Green Soup 122
Sambals
    Chinchalok with Chillies 61
    Green Chilli Sambal 55
    Mango Sambal 55
    Sambal Belacan 61
    Sambal Belacan Brinjals 60
    Sambal Bendi 62
    Sambal Goreng Udang 54
    Sambal Heh Bee 57
    Sambal Ikan 58, 59
    Sambal Ikan Bilis 57
    Sambal Ikan Sumbat 58
    Sambal Timun and Nanas 60
    Sambal Tumis Kerang 56
    Sambal Udang Goreng Assam 56
    Sambal Udang Petai 63
Sar Keong Chicken/Duck 66
Screwpine Leaves 12
Seafood
    Assam Fish 82
    Chilli Fish 82
    Fresh Anchovy Fry Omelette 87
    Fried Anchovies with Groundnuts 87
    Fried Ikan Bawal Putih with Taucheong 89
    Heh Kian 25
    Ikan Assam Pedas 86

Ikan Cencaru Sumbat   88
Ikan Kuning   86
Ikan Masak Assam Kichap   83
Ikan Panggang   83, 84
Ikan Pari Fried Kiam Chai   82
Kiam Hu Branda   29
Kiam Hu Char   83
Pee Hu Char   86
Sambal Ikan Sumbat   58
Sweet Sour Crab   80, 81
Sweet Sour Fish   81
Sengkuang Koon Th'ng   118
Serikaya   129, 130
Sesame Seeds   12
Shrimp Paste   12, 60, 61
Siamese Laksa   104
Slaked Lime   12, 134
Sotong Fried Kin Chai   95
Soups
    Bayam Th,ng   123
    Hu Peow Pig's Intestine Soup   119
    Hu Peow Th'ng   119, 120
    Kiam Chai Arp   117
    Mee Suar Soup   123
    Pau Hu Th'ng   116
    Poh Ho Th'ng   122
    Prawns Balls in Cabbage Soup   122
    Roasted Pork and Mustard Green Soup   122
    Salt Fish and Soya Bean Soup   118
    Sengkuang Koon Th'ng   118
    Spare Ribs in Preserved Soya Bean Soup   123
    Transparent Vermicelli and Fish Ball Soup   118
Soya Bean Cake
    Fried Soya Bean Cake and Long Beans   94
    Fried Stuffed Taukua   28
    Salt Fish Soya Bean Soup   118
Soya Bean Paste   13
    Bah Yew Pho in Taucheong   74
    Fried Brinjals and Soya Bean Paste   92
    Fried Ikan Bawal Putih with Taucheong   29
    La La Fried in Taucheong   29
    Spare Ribs in Preserved Soya Bean Soup   123
Spareribs in Preserved Soya Bean Soup   123
Spinach
    Bayam Masak Lemak   94
    Bayam Th'ng   123
Steamed Pulut and White Beans   136
Sweet Potato
    Bubur Cha Cha   127
Sweet Potato Leaves
    Daun Ubi Keledek Masak Lemak   95
Sweet Sour Crab   80, 81
Sweet Sour Fish   81
Sweet Sour Spareribs   76

Tamarind Pieces   13
Tamarind Pulp   13
Tapioca
    Chopadak Ubi Kayu   137
    Kuih Bengka Ubi Kayu   132
    Tapioca in Sweet Gravy   132
Taucheong
    (See Soya Bean Paste)
Taugeh
    (See Bean Sprouts)
Transparent Vermicelli and Fish Ball Soup   118
Taukua
    (See Soya Bean Cake)
Tau Yew Bak   77

Vegetables
    Bayam Masak Lemak   94
    Beef Fried with Cauliflower   95
    Chap Chai Lemak   92
    Daun Ubi Keledek Masak Lemak   95
    Egg and Cucumber Kerabu   101
    Fried Brinjals in Soya Bean Paste   92
    Fried Kangkong or Long Beans with Dried Prawns   97
    Fried Salt Fish with Taugeh   94
    Fried Soya Bean Cake and Long Beans   94
    Jiu Hu Char with Sengkuang   96
    Kerabu Taugeh   101
    Kerang Kucai Goreng   92, 93
    Kobis Masak Lemak (1)   100
    Kobis Masak Lemak (2)   100
    Nyonya Chap Chai 97, 98
    Sotong Fried Kin Chai   95
Vermicelli
    Transparent Vermicelli and Fish Ball Soup   118

Water Convolvulus
    Fried Kangkong or Long Beans with Dried Prawns   97
White Beans
    Steamed Pulut with White Beans   136
Yam
    Bubur Cha Cha   127
Yambean
    Jiu Hu Char with Sengkuang   96
    Po Piah   30, 31
    Po Piah Chien   31
    Sengkuang Koon Th'ng   118